STATUES WITHOUT SHADOWS

Anna's parents should never have met. He was the son of down-at-heel aristocrats; she was the child of a mining family. In 1950s London, they inhabited an idealistic but brittle world of writers and journalists. Anna was born in 1960, as their marriage was falling apart. By the age of seven, both her parents were dead. Brought up by her grandparents, believing her mother had died of cancer and her father of pneumonia, it wasn't until her late twenties that Anna uncovered the disturbing truth about her parents' glittering and early lives.

ANNA SWAN

STATUES WITHOUT SHADOWS

A daughter's search for the truth about
the parents she never knew

Complete and Unabridged

ULVERSCROFT
Leicester

First published in Great Britain in 2005 by
Hodder and Stoughton
a division of
Hodder Headline
London

First Large Print Edition
published 2006
by arrangement with
Hodder Headline
London

British Library CIP Data

Swan, Anna, 1960 –
Statues without shadows: a daughter's search for the
truth about the parents she never knew.—
Large print ed.—
Ulverscroft large print series: non-fiction
1. Swan, Anna, 1960 – 2. Orphans—Great Britain
—Biography 3. Children of suicide victims—Great
Britain—Biography 4. Adult children—Psychology
5. Large type books
I. Title
362.7′3′092

ISBN 1–84617–407–4

Published by
F. A. Thorpe (Publishing)
Anstey, Leicestershire
Set by Words & Graphics Ltd.
Anstey, Leicestershire
Printed and bound in Great Britain by
T. J. International Ltd., Padstow, Cornwall

This book is printed on acid-free paper

For
Finetta Hemming, Esmé and Andy Marino
(snr), Maggie O'Keefe, Sidney Owen and
Klaus and Ursula Philips — who welcomed
me into their families and made me feel
like one of their own

Contents

Acknowledgements

My sincere thanks to my agent, Andrew Lownie, and the Biographers' Club, for unwavering support and faith in the book; everyone at Hodder and Stoughton, particularly my editor, Helen Coyle, for constant encouragement and judicious feedback, and to Emma Heyworth-Dunn for commissioning the book, Lucy Bennett, Juliet Brightmore, Jocasta Brownlee, Jacqui Lewis, Susan Liu, Morag Lyall and Rowena Webb.

For their generosity and invaluable help with research, I would like to thank Sonia Allen, Al Alvarez, David Attenborough, Rowley Atterbury, Dot Barclay, Gordana Batinica, Sebastian Beaumont, Rosamond Belfrage, Sue Blake, Eileen Brooksbank, Peter Burton, Vicki and Barry Clark, Jim Cochrane, Bob Cole, Doris Collins, Terence Cooper, Iliana Cranston, Amy Creighton, Tony and Sarah Curtis, Richard Davenport-Hines, Jennifer Dee, Catherine Dupré, Godfrey Evans, Tucker Finlayson, Paddy Fraser, Stephen Gardiner, Rosemary Goad, Jane Goff, Alex Gollner, Richard Gollner, Norman Goodman, Lyndall Gordon, Richard Gordon,

Roy Greenslade, Michael Gribble, Christopher Hawtree, Sheena Hewitt, Penny Hoare, Paul Hoffman, Neil Hornick, Gerald Howells, Howard and Marsli Howells, Deborah Jaffe, Joan Johnson, Marigold Johnson, Edward Kenney, Francis King, Tomorr Kokona, Jeremy Lewis, David Lincoln-Howells, Mary Lovell, Grahame Matthews, John Mayes, Paul Maylam, Amalie Niland, Kathy Perutz, Claudia Philips, Deborah Philips, Tom Pitchon, David Platzer, Marlene Powell, Isabel Quigly, Michael Ratcliffe, Elizabeth Rosenberg, Pamela and Victor Round, Jupi Sen, Sheila Sen, Susan Shaw, Rachel Speight, Natasha Spender, Charles Sprawson, Juana Subercaseaux, Paz Subercaseaux, Caroline Swan, Noreen Taylor, Raleigh Trevelyan, Anne Valery, Pauline Welsh, Tom Wicker, Hugh Williams, Peregrine Worsthorne, and the Boys at the LRB.

My thanks to those who have sadly died since I began writing this book, their contributions and support made all the difference: Neville Braybrooke, Susan Hill, Antje Johnson, Ray Oliver, Anthony Rhodes, Anthony Sampson, John Swan and Tony Tighe.

And to Andy Marino for priceless editorial expertise, and so much more.

Prologue

My parents were both writers. Michael Swan was born in 1923 into an aristocratic, artistic family in Kensington, and died in 1967 in a squalid bed-sit in Shepherd's Bush. Joan Swan, *née* Howells, was born in 1931 in Merthyr Tydfil, South Wales; her forebears were coal miners. She died in Worcester Royal Infirmary in 1962 when I was a baby.

I first heard the word orphan applied to me when I went to boarding school at the age of ten. As the new girls filed into the dormitory, kitted out in our grey tunics and ankle socks, I heard the housemistress whisper, 'Look, there's the poor little orphan.' She was pointing at me and I was mortified. It had never crossed my mind that I was the embodiment of Dickensian deprivation, a wretched and woeful Olivia Twist. It was my first encounter with pity and I didn't like it one bit.

As a grown-up, I still cringe at the word and never use it, mostly because it says only one thing about me. There's a hard-earned pride in having overcome adversity, but the desire to brand oneself baffles me. Not long ago I ran into an American acquaintance whom I hadn't seen for about eight years. He was wearing a badge that declared in loud red lettering: 'I'm a survivor.' It came with his recent membership of Alcoholics Anonymous, along with the need to broadcast his recovery. I'm all for transparency but labels such as survivor and, worst of all, victim, advertise damaged goods and little else. It's the equivalent of me carrying a banner that reads: 'Abandoned'.

I grew up with my maternal grandparents believing my mother was the saint and my father the villain. These labels only obscured and diminished them. Over the years I was given tiny scraps of information which I kept locked away like treasure: my mother liked dark chocolate and green olives, she loved Chopin and Edith Piaf and her favourite tree was the weeping willow. I heard almost nothing about my father other than that he'd written a few books, he was 'ill in the head' and that he and his relatives were 'a bunch of toffs'. Apparently, I was better off without them. I wouldn't see them again until I was twenty, when I decided I was old enough to make up my own mind.

Grandma told me my mother died of cancer when I was a baby and my father of pneumonia when I was seven. These white lies were well meant, but as I grew older I realised that certain members of my maternal family were unacquainted with emotional honesty, preferring to seethe silently rather than own up to the grubby truth. The lid on our particular can of worms remained firmly in place until I was twenty-eight, when I stole a quick look inside then carefully closed it again for more than a decade.

★　★　★

Against Grandpa's better judgement, in 1951 my grandparents moved from Merthyr Tydfil to London, where they were caretakers of two residential buildings in Hyde Park Gardens, near Marble Arch. Grandma was a compulsive cleaner and rarely without her Pledge and yellow duster. Our basement flat was spotless; the furniture was Utility and the rugs acrylic, polished and hoovered down to their grain and weft. Hidden but pervasive, the mess my parents left behind was swept under the family carpet.

Frailty and poor health, however, were fully endorsed and even encouraged. With a few exceptions, ours is a sick family. From

3

nervous breakdowns, depression, addictions and hypochondria to cancer, kidney disease and carpal tunnel syndrome, hospitalisation and surgery are rife. I got off lightly with insomnia and a spinal condition.

In an atmosphere thick with evasion and sanitised with Dettol and TCP, any questions I had about my parents were quickly stifled. I asked only once about their friends. Grandma shuddered and said, 'They're not nice people.' 'Not nice' was a euphemism I didn't understand at the time. I learned to fall in line with the stoical silence and stopped asking about my parents, but I was aware of the blame resolutely aimed at my father and anyone associated with him.

Culpability was often misattributed in our family, as though there were no grey area between guilt and innocence. It was never acknowledged, but three of Grandma's four children were somewhat remiss in their responsibilities as parents. At various times, she was left holding the babies; the last was my cousin Justin, but by then Grandma was nearly seventy. He was nine months old when he was taken into care and adopted.

Like me, my cousin David was passed around during his first few years, but Grandma didn't have enough love to go round: I got the majority, David got the dregs. At the age of five, he went to live with his father — my mother's younger brother — and his new wife. They were more Addams Family than the Waltons, to the extent that I stopped using their real names years ago: I renamed them Morticia and Gomez, and their home Castle Greyskull. I haven't set foot in the Castle since 1997.

★ ★ ★

As a child I'd been given a jigsaw puzzle made up of whispered rumours and half-truths. The older I became the less I wanted to know, my curiosity choked by teenage embarrassment and, by my early twenties, fear of what I might find out about my parents *and* myself; the creeping thoughts at the back of my mind were that I might inherit my father's mental illness or die young like my mother. The missing pieces held little attraction for me, or rather they were too big to contemplate. Besides, I had no idea where to find them and even less how to fit them all together.

Until I was twenty-eight I had no reason to distrust my grandparents' account, thread-bare as it was, but a chance remark from one of my cousins — on the 'wrong' side of the family, as Grandma would have put it

— revealed a vital deception: my father hadn't died of pneumonia. Not knowing what to do with it I kept the news to myself. A year or so later I discovered my mother's death was a mirror-image of his. It took me nearly fifteen years to expose the rest of the fiction.

That first revelation triggered my writing career. It made me curious about my father and I wondered if he might have left me a dormant literary legacy. I wrote a few short stories — thankfully they never saw print — and had a couple of poems published. It was 1988, near the end of a culturally and politically ambivalent decade: a collage of acid house and indie ravers mixing with poll tax protesters heading for Trafalgar Square, council houses and nationalised industries both up for sale at knock-down prices and Kylie and Jason cheeping up the charts. I didn't have to look too far for inspiration; it was right there within my own family. I believed I had the makings of a novel: romantic plot, glamorous characters, post-war setting, exotic locations. My investigations were half-hearted, in part because I was ill-equipped to pursue what lay behind the truth but also because my parents' story was non-stop drama — and I only knew the half of it at that point. It didn't work as a novel because I felt the reader would be left thinking: that could never happen in real life. I followed a few leads, wrote three or four scrappy chapters then gave in without much of a fight. I wasn't quite curious enough.

It wasn't until four years ago, when I began writing this book, that my entire outlook shifted. I'd underplayed my parents' significance with good reason, but in avoiding the past I did all three of us a disservice. It was far easier to dismiss their influence than examine it, but what worked for me as a child wasn't doing me any favours as an adult. I got by just fine but my confidence was precarious and my writing no more than adequate. Most of all, my love life was a mess and I wasn't bold enough to find out why. Having bypassed my fears of clinical depression and a premature death, at thirty-nine I was finally grown-up enough to confront my parents with all my unvoiced questions.

Like a detective working on a cold case, I was compelled to hunt down the evidence and uncover the perjury. Following a paper trail of long-closed files, court documents, archived correspondence and love letters, I know my parents more intimately than if they were here to tell me their secrets. Ultimately it was the witnesses and bystanders, their allegedly 'not nice' friends, who helped me fill in the details and arrive at some kind of conclusion.

The picture may never be complete, but as the pieces of my parents' lives fell into place I saw them in their true light, and it was even darker than I imagined. I decoded the euphemisms, unravelled fact from fiction and finally discovered who my parents really were and what drove them to their early deaths. The charges of sainthood and villainy don't do them justice.

1

Upstairs Downstairs

Home was a movable feast, or rather famine. After my mother died in September 1962, I lived with my grandparents for about six months. During this time there were various options under consideration: Auntie Vera in Merthyr offered to adopt me, as did Uncle Howard and his wife Marsli; my grandparents wanted to keep me; and my father, unable to take care of himself let alone a toddler, planned to hand me over to my godparents. Had I been aware of all these potential destinations, I might have felt like lost luggage with a tag tied to my wrist saying: 'Where does this child belong?' No one seemed to know, except me. At the custody trial instigated by my father against my grandparents, on 27 March 1963, the court decided on the worst possible solution. It was three months after my second birthday, and had the judge asked me the crucial question I would have pointed to Grandma. The law proved itself an ass, and in the long run everyone lost out.

What little security I had was wrapped up in my grandparents and the safest place in the world was their kitchen at Hyde Park Gardens. Hidden below ground level, it was warm in winter and cool in summer, but I felt protected from more than the elements. One of my earliest memories is of sitting in Grandma's lap as she knitted a cardi, a three-bar electric fire close by; her feet were always cold and chilblains was one of the first big words I learned. With her arms around me I'd watch her knit one, purl one. She couldn't follow complicated patterns so she made them up as she went along: Grandma liked things plain and simple.

She had big brown eyes the colour of melting chocolate and the sweetest smile; it was a face made for gazing at grandchildren, the ones she favoured anyway. Despite her poor circulation, her hands were always warm, no doubt because they were never still. I loved the feel of her stroking me; 'Rub my tummy,' was one of my most frequent bedtime requests. I believed I was out of harm's way, unaware that I was about to be wrenched from Grandma's arms by court order.

From March 1963, the following two years or so were the unhappiest of my childhood. I was old enough to know I was in the wrong place and that there was something a bit odd about the people who were supposed to be taking care of me. Everything seemed over-sized and menacing, from the brown Bentley in the drive to the back garden running wild with children shrieking and fighting. I didn't understand why I was there but I vaguely recall being told that this was now my home and I had to make the best of it.

The older children were shouty and scary, but I liked the little girl called Gabrielle. She had curly red hair and freckles and was about the same age as me. When we played doctors and nurses the bigger children made me be the patient because I was the smallest. They pinched and prodded me, but when I said I didn't like it, one of them yelled, 'We're the boss in this house.' I don't remember much about the grown-ups, but the man smelled of cigarettes and was tall and bendy, with a pointy nose and bushy eyebrows: he seemed like a wicked magician with a nasty trick up his sleeve.

Whenever I looked out of the window the sky was full of clouds, as though winter lasted all year long. Like splintered frost, fragments of memories stick in my mind: shivering in a cold bathroom, playing with a doll behind a sofa while I hid from the other children, and eating a lot of crisps and Mars Bars — I didn't like the layer of toffee and I vividly recall sticking out my tongue as I smeared the gooey bit on the back of a chair when no one was looking. It ought to have been all jolly japes and lashings of ginger beer, but left to our own devices it was more *Lord of the Flies* than *The Famous Five*.

At some point I figured out the grown-ups were my god-parents, Alan and Dina Barnsley. They had promised my father he could see me whenever he liked; their home was his home. Initially, the arrangement seemed to work but his visits became more and more infrequent. By the end of 1965, he was as unwelcome here as he was at Hyde Park Gardens.

The Barnsleys talked funny and they sounded nothing like my grandparents. I don't recall what we ate, only that we sat at a big table and the food was different from Grandma's dinners served up in the kitchen. There were lots of books and board games and we went to church a lot. The smell of church made me feel sick and we had to keep quiet and pretend to be serious, though I wasn't very good at either. There were walks by the river and we played hide-and-seek in a spooky monastery, where I did more hiding than seeking. What I liked best was that we didn't have to have a bath too often.

My grandparents were occasionally allowed to visit. I remember sitting on the back seat of their Morris Minor with Grandma spitting on her hankie in a vain attempt to remove the ingrained dirt from my hands and neck. For a woman with a compulsion for hygiene my grimy clothes and unwashed hair were an affront: not only had the Barnsleys taken her daughter's only child from her, they didn't even bother to keep me clean.

I sensed my time in the chilly, disorderly house wasn't for ever and that if I wished for it with all my heart I'd end up where I belonged. I didn't know it then but the arrangement with the Barnsleys had backfired and it was my father who unintentionally caused it. As if I'd found a pair of ruby slippers and clicked my heels together three times, my wish suddenly came true. I've believed in happy endings ever since.

★   ★   ★

I was almost five when I was made a Ward of Court. I had no idea what it meant, nor did I care: all that mattered was that I was back in our warm and cosy basement. Around this time I realised that my circumstances were at odds with my new friends at primary school.

13

Even the television told me I was different. It was the mid 1960s and my onscreen playmates were Andy Pandy, Twizzle and the Flowerpot Men, broadcast under the heading *Watch with Mother*. Unable to abide by the BBC's imperative, I watched alone. Likewise, the last Sunday in March singled me out. At school we made Mother's Day cards decorated with hearts and flowers, but mine was written to Grandma.

She may have looked out of place standing at the school gates alongside the mums with their bouffant hairdos and false eyelashes, white go-go boots and American Tan tights, but she wouldn't have been conscious of it. Unembarrassable and oblivious to current trends, she had her own sense of style, as illustrated by her collection of hats. The most exceptional looked like a beehive made of black wool loops hung with plastic gold discs that jingled when she walked. For Grandma's generation, fashion gave way to comfort and convenience: polyester blouses, with no frills or flounces, and Terylene slacks — she never called them trousers — with elasticated waistbands or a rayon slip showing below the hem of her Crimplene frock. She crackled with static electricity, but having grown up with the harsh laundry demands of wool and cotton she was a big fan of synthetics and her bywords were drip-dry and easycare.

At home she wore a pink bri-nylon housecoat to protect her clothes. Aside from the occasional home-made dessert and her crispy chips, cooking had never been her forte. Dinners were baked beans on burned toast, Fray Bentos steak pie and lumpy mash or fish fingers and peas. Spaghetti came in a tin and Heinz Salad Cream accompanied limp lettuce with sliced beetroot and cucumber pickled in sugar and Sarson's vinegar. She didn't have the time or inclination for baking. Cakes were shop-bought but she made the most perfect rice pudding, so milky you had to drink it. Fruit didn't feature much, except for tinned peaches with Carnation condensed milk and clementines at Christmas.

Grandma couldn't care less what people thought of her culinary deficiencies or eccentric headwear; her concerns were far more deeply rooted. She was a born worrier, always anticipating the worst and in thrall to everyone else's ailments, as though illness or injury marked you as special. We used to visit family in South Wales every summer, but the sky over Merthyr was rarely sunny. Even their homes had a funereal atmosphere, as if a close relative had just passed away. The aunties would gather in dimly lit corridors, their hushed conversation accompanied by a cup of tea and a slice of soda cake as they savoured details of the latest casualty: *Your Life in their Hands* and *Emergency Ward Ten* had nothing on the Howells family. A solitary sneeze or a momentary cough were enough to set Grandma checking for symptoms of TB or diphtheria. Her own health came second, but she was a slave to her pills: white to calm her nerves, yellow to sleep and blue to wake her up in the morning.

As an insomniac she had many more hours in the day to fill, but few were allocated to leisure. I remember once waking up at about midnight and wandering past the bathroom where Grandma was on her knees scrubbing the lino. When she wasn't hoovering or dusting or washing clothes in the kitchen sink, she was stitching a dropped hem or varnishing a cupboard door. She was far too industrious for hobbies but seemed to take pleasure in DIY. Whenever there was a little money to spare she would decorate. I remember the plasticky smell of Fablon — in lipstick red or lemon yellow — as she relined the kitchen shelves yet again, and the disaster when she painted our front door in forest green gloss so thick it never really dried. She was happiest up a ladder with a brush and a bucket of paste, as if papering over the cracks in our afflicted family.

Grandpa was harder to fathom. A wraith-like presence with enormous ears and a shiny bald head, I never heard his key in the lock or the door slam, he just seemed to materialise from elsewhere. He didn't talk much. It wasn't that he didn't have anything to say — you could sense a sharp mind at work behind his bright blue eyes — but he didn't feel the need to share it. His interior world was a busy but private place.

Grandma's accent had almost faded after more than a decade in London, but Grandpa defiantly held on to his own as though he were passing time until he could go home to Merthyr. What little he said was worth waiting for, especially when he used naughty words. In his sing-song lilt, 'There's bloody marvellous,' or 'A proper silly cow she is,' sounded like poetry to me. I once asked him, 'Why do you go to the barber if you haven't got any hair?' 'Cheeky bugger,' he said. He sometimes sang me a song from his boyhood to the tune of the Welsh battle anthem 'Men of Harlech'. The opening lines were: 'I'm a man who came from Scotland/Shooting peas up a nanny-goat's bottom/I'm a man who came from Scotland shooting pcas away.' While I grinned with delight, Grandma tutted, 'Alf, you daft apeth.'

As if he were saving them up for later, his mischievous moments were rationed. Grandma was the voice in the family and she more than made up for his quiet contemplation. She also had appearances to keep up and did her grocery shopping at Marks and Sparks and Selfridges Food Hall, a twenty-minute walk up the Bayswater Road to Oxford Street. She wouldn't be caught dead at the nearby Co-op; quality counted, no matter that it cost a few pence more.

She'd complain about the dirt and volume of people — 'Filthy with germs they are' — but secretly I think she liked the crowds. She could strike up a conversation at the drop of one of her outrageous hats and would relay intimate details of our on-going family misfortunes: her youngest daughter's anaemia brought on by heavy periods, her brother-in-law's flatulence or her own constipation and which brand of suppository she was currently prescribed. Forsaking clarity for discretion, these complaints were moderated as 'women's trouble', 'wind' and 'bunged up below'; Grandma rarely told it like it was.

While she thrived on the exhaust fumes of the capital's traffic, Grandpa silently pined for the honest pollution of the Valleys. It was life's small pleasures that mattered to him, such as checking the football pools or reading the *Merthyr Express* with a saucer of cooling tea at his elbow and a pipe in his hand. He kept his tobacco in a black leather pouch that smelled like roasting coffee beans and Ovaltine. Sitting in his armchair gazing into the distance, the air around him was as dense as the mist surrounding his beloved Brecon Beacons.

It was an adequate marriage at best, with anniversaries measured by sickness and loss rather than joy and celebration. Grandpa wasn't the tactile type and I never saw my grandparents hold hands or exchange any affection, but nor did I hear them argue; bicker perhaps, but there was rarely any shouting. After forty years together there wasn't much of an alternative but to put up with each other. As for Grandpa, it all seemed to pass him by: he worked, he slept, he ate, and was partial to kippers and Madeira cake. But in his early sixties, he was rushed to St Mary's Hospital with ruptured ulcers and lost two-thirds of his stomach. While Grandma unburdened her sorrows to the stranger at the bus stop or the salesman at the front door, her reserved and watchful husband took it all in, and kept it there.

Our neighbours, or rather employers, at Hyde Park Gardens included the Duchess of

Roxburghe and Lady Sutherland. Grandpa often took me up in the service elevator to keep the nobility company. I was the cheeky little chatterbox caught between floors with a double-barrelled first name, Anna-Petra, and an accent that didn't fit below stairs.

My favourite neighbour was Lady Butlin, a beautiful blonde who rarely got out of bed. When I went to visit her after school, her maid would bring in a tray with milk and fancy chocolate biscuits for me and a glass of amber-coloured liquid which I assumed was Lady Butlin's medicine. I'd sit beside her on slippery, turquoise satin sheets as we read *The Tales of Beatrix Potter* together. We liked the Flopsy Bunnies and Tom Kitten best. Her medicine seemed to make her sad, and sometimes she cried when I had to go back downstairs for tea. Years later I discovered she was the widow of the holiday camp king and a bed-ridden alcoholic.

Unlike me, my grandparents knew their place. When the Duchess of Roxburghe entertained, everything came to a halt down in the basement as Grandma fussed with a damp tea towel, pressing the trousers of Grandpa's smart black suit and brushing imaginary dust from the lapels of his jacket. With his tie in a Windsor knot under an immaculate white collar, he served as doorman to peers of the realm, MPs and captains of industry and their glamorous wives. Grandpa was respectful and courteous to the aristocracy and Establishment decked out in their mink stoles and tuxedos, but if he'd had a forelock he would never have tugged it: his Celtic pride wouldn't let him. The Welsh don't defer to anyone, least of all the English.

My father's family was as well bred as the residents upstairs, but by now penurious. In Grandma's book breeding didn't count for much, unless you were rich. Besides, the Swans were 'arty types'. She had fixed ideas about who was respectable and who wasn't, and they were firmly on the wrong side of the divide. Authority figures such as the family doctor or the bank manager automatically earned her regard: those were proper, decent jobs. She didn't use words such as 'louche' or 'unsavoury', but considered the Swans morally dubious. Somehow it was acceptable for me to spend unsupervised visits upstairs with a woman who was drunk by teatime, but my paternal relatives were a bad lot.

Grandma's disapproval was covert and the unspoken animosity persuasive. 'What are you looking at that for?' she said when she caught me reading a book my father had given me called *Exploring the Arts*. I put it back on the shelf and didn't open it again for years. Without saying it out loud, she insinuated that any gift from him was tainted. A tiny part of me felt sorry for him, but I kept any allegiance with my father to myself.

Grandpa read his *Merthyr Express* and the *News of the World* and Grandma occasionally flicked through *Woman's Realm*, but I never saw either of them read a book. Grandma liked the televised wrestling on a Saturday afternoon. Compelled by the potential for injury, she refused to believe the violence was staged. 'Shockin' it is, shockin'!' she would shout at the screen as Mick McManus and Jackie Pallo appeared to dislocate each other's body parts with a flying snap kick or a cobra slam. Grandpa preferred *Z Cars* and *Dixon of Dock Green*. Much to my frustration, I wasn't allowed to watch *Monty Python* or even *Magpie, Blue Peter*'s more culturally alert counterpart. Grandma's blanket phrase for the subversive or avant-garde was 'Rude and nasty it is.' She associated anything arty or literary with my father. Over-cautious in trying to protect me from his intellectual influence, she labelled most things outside her experience as suspect. Grandpa didn't have much to say either way.

Worst of all, I didn't talk like anyone else in

the family. When I said words such as 'water' or 'butter' Grandma would tease: 'Ooh, there's la-de-da for you.' My father and the Barnsleys had left their mark and I'd ended up posh. Over the years I learned to tone it down a notch or two. The conflict between Grandma and my father was in some ways subtle and in others blatant. It seemed I had to choose a side. With no one to defend him, my father didn't stand a chance. Grandma won that round and did her best to delay the inevitable but I think she knew I was never quite hers.

2

Hyde by Name and Nature

On the surface, my parents' childhoods were relatively secure. Each grew up with two parents and three siblings but without much money. In their different ways they were both undermined by maternal dominance, while their pipe-smoking fathers paid the bills and kept to themselves.

By the time my father was born, in 1923, the family was no longer affluent or titled. Growing up in rented accommodation in Kensington, he must have found it hard to relate to a lineage dating back to the landed gentry of the twelfth century: Robin Hood would have been more real to him than his earliest known ancestor, Matthew, Lord de Hyde. Born c.1167 and of Norman stock, he was a *grand fromage* in the enforcement of the feudal system on the Saxon populace and loyal to Richard the Lion-Heart. This is all that's known of de Hyde except that, with cinematic licence, he may have swashed and buckled and even accompanied the King on the Third Crusade (1190–1192). In order to raise ready money for the venture, Richard sold offices and titles, the Plantagenet equivalent of cash for questions.

Among the most memorable and influential of my father's ancestors was Edward Hyde (1609–74), or Steady Eddie as I've come to think of him. His friend Samuel Pepys made seventy-three references to him in his *Diary*, and proclaimed he was 'mad in love with him' for his ease and authority in public speaking. He was also a skilled diplomat and in 1661, a year after the Restoration, Edward was made first Earl of Clarendon for services to the crown. By now Chief Minister and confidant to Charles II, Edward dominated parliament for seven years. Obstinate, upstanding and outspoken, he was no sycophant and it almost cost him his head. Under pressure from a cabal of self-promoting ministers, in 1667 the King charged him with treason for, among other things, his criticisms of the royal lifestyle, including Charles' flagrant displays of adultery. The charge was soon dropped but Edward was irrevocably out of favour and went into exile in France, where he died at the age of sixty-five. His body was eventually returned to England and buried at Westminster Abbey.

In 1659 his daughter Anne married James,

Duke of York, later James II. They had eight children, all of whom died young except Mary who ruled jointly with William III, and Anne who also became Queen. The royal line ended when she died in 1714 and the crown passed to the House of Hanover. For the Hydes it was downhill all the way to Bohemia, via commerce and the colonies. The motto on their coat of arms, 'Soyez Ferme' (Be Steadfast), was fading. Somewhere along the descent the blue blood had mixed with bad blood. By a quirk of fate, I grew up in Hyde Park Gardens, perpendicular to Clarendon Street, ignorant of the ancestral connection yet subconsciously alert to Steady Eddie's mandate.

The family seat was Hyde Hall near Stockport, Cheshire, built during Elizabeth I's reign. An eighteenth-century painting portrays a pastoral scene of rolling acres behind the mansion and well-tended gardens sloping towards a millstream, its most vital asset. As the Hydes expanded their business interests — primarily farming and domestic spinning and weaving — and built housing for its labour force, the surrounding area took on the family name. With the potential for water power from its fast-flowing streams and the nearby River Tame, by the end of the century the developments of the Industrial

Revolution had transformed the quiet agricultural community into a thriving town famous for its cotton and silk production.

The Hydes left Cheshire for Somerset in 1857 when coal seams were discovered under the site of the original Hall. A decade later it was described in an unattributed document as 'no longer a place of refinement, the stream in front of the house runs with pollution, its waters being of nearly every colour, owing to the offensive discharges from the factories'. A metaphor for the bad blood or a premonition of urban decay, the contamination spread and the Hall was demolished in 1867. All that remains of the family's influence is the town's name.

The Hydes enjoyed centuries of wealth and power interrupted by scandal and disgrace. When a later Anne Hyde married George Clarke, who was to be appointed Lieutenant-Governor of New York in 1736, they joined names. A succession of American George Hyde-Clarkes acquired various nicknames, including George 'The Ne'er Do Well'. A bounder and a slave trader, in 1777 he inherited a sugar plantation in the West Indies from a bachelor uncle, and promptly deserted his wife and children to elope with his mistress to Jamaica.

George 'The Builder' reconstructed Hyde

Hall in 6,000 acres of land overlooking Otsego Lake in Cooperstown, upstate New York. His son, George 'The Bankrupt', was a notorious gambler and reprobate, a dashing wastrel more interested in stocking his wine cellar and dandy's wardrobe than keeping the books in order. In 1887 he lost the entire estate of $1 million, at the time the biggest bankruptcy in American history. In what was perhaps a pre-emptive move, his heir George 'The Gentleman' married into money and bought back the Hall and 3,000 acres.

The last George was 'The Recluse', but the Hyde-Clarke vigour, as well as the cash, had finally run out. He died in 1955 leaving the Hall in ramshackle disrepair. It stood derelict for the next nine years, with seedlings sprouting through broken windows and a grand piano rotting in an outhouse, its only residents vermin and snakes. In 1963 the fifty-room mansion passed to the state of New York. The following year the Friends of Hyde Hall acquired the uninhabitable building of collapsed ceilings and decaying staircases. The Friends raised and invested over $1 million for renovation, and it's now a museum to Cooperstown's colonial past, its income derived from private donations, corporate events and summer concerts. The

portraits of long-dead Georges hang throughout the Hall, some steadfast, some not.

★   ★   ★

I knew almost nothing about my father's side
of the family until I was twenty, and much of
the history was news to me when Uncle John,
my father's older brother, began investigating
our ancestry in earnest about ten years ago.
Crikey, I thought, that's one hell of a legacy
to live up to. Consistently déclassé, we've
rather let the side down.

I often wonder how my father felt about
our royal past. I suspect he would have been
quietly amused. Uncle John, however, took it
very seriously; it seems the blue blood,
diluted as it is, runs deeper in some of us
than others. John was by turns earthy and
snooty, generous and stingy. He liked a pint
or three of Chiswick bitter at his local pub in
Ealing, but deplored Estuary English; he
would never let me pay for lunch but
penny-pinched when it came to the tip and
I'd have to sneak the waitress an extra couple
of quid. Entertaining and exasperating,
broad-minded and judgemental, he had an
opinion on everything and was always up for
a good argument. It took me a long time to
figure out but Uncle John and my father were

as alike and contrary as fraternal peas in a pod.

The aristocratic pedigree came from my grandmother, Gwendolyn Hyde-Clarke. John's genealogical research included thirteen files on the Hydes, and one sketchy page on the Swans. His father Edwin, a portrait painter known to everyone as Topsy, was born in 1873 in Ballyragget, Ireland. His forebears were doctors and clergy. Topsy's father, Robert Lafayette Swan, was President of the Royal College of Surgeons. He published several texts on sexually transmitted diseases and in 1876 founded the Rotunda Orthopaedic Hospital in Dublin. As a doctor himself, I was surprised John showed such scant interest in his paternal line since he adored his father and barely tolerated his mother. When I asked him he said, 'The Hydes are much more interesting than the Swans.' Interesting was a loaded word, and in this case it meant accomplished, connected and well-bred.

John was as complex a character as my father. With their striking profiles and shiny, fair hair they shared identikit features and colouring, but my father was long-legged and lean like a middle-distance runner while John was short and stocky. He often joked that my father had the hands of a pianist while his looked like a pound of sausages. Both were single-minded and ambitious but their sensibilities were at odds. John was brusque and pragmatic, my father sensitive and cerebral, but neither of Topsy's sons inherited his happy-go-lucky outlook.

Too squeamish for medicine and too sceptical for the cloth, at the tail-end of the Impressionist period, Topsy and his older brother Cuthbert studied art at the Académie Julian in Paris. Topsy was a sympathetic and subtle painter and had a gift for revealing his subjects' temperaments as much as their physical characteristics. His brush strokes are strong and sure but the illumination around his sitters muted and diffuse. I was curious about the shadowy quality as it didn't seem to fit his personality. Initially I assumed it was because until the early 1920s he would have worked by gaslight, its low lit radiance more subdued than electricity's cold glare.

Topsy had one artistic weakness: he couldn't paint hands and usually hid them in pockets or gloves or beneath the folds of a shawl. In a self-portrait painted in his fifties, he's every inch the artist in his black beret, floppy bow-tie and round spectacles — and he's holding a brush in what almost resembles a thumb and forefinger. His expression is serene but knowing, as though he's owning up to his shortcoming. He exhibited at the Royal Academy, the Royal Institute of Painters and in the provinces, and among his best-known subjects were G.K. Chesterton and Field Marshall Montgomery. Devoted to his family and his profession, Topsy was content with his lot; he knew he was never going to rank among the great masters, but he loved his work and that was enough.

I was always eager to hear John talk about his father, in part because he was such an enthusiastic storyteller but in later years it distracted him from his depression. Towards the end of his life John was in and out of hospital, but knee and hip replacements were the least of it: more than once, he checked himself into the local psychiatric ward. Whenever he was in low spirits or fretful, I'd say, 'Tell me about Topsy.' His face would light up and his anxieties temporarily disappear.

I never heard my father's memories of Topsy; by the time I was old enough to listen his mind and recall were already lost. In his place, John became my conduit to the past. Despite a seepage of facts and rerouting of certain information, when it came to Topsy I could tell John felt no need to divert from the truth. When he was about fourteen, Topsy asked him to accompany him on a walk in Kensington Gardens. 'He wanted to have a fatherly talk, and after several minutes of coughs and false starts he finally asked me if I knew about the birds and the bees. 'Of course,' I replied. 'That's all right then,' he said, 'but no hanky-panky before marriage.' That was all the advice he had on the matter.'

Principled and strait-laced, Topsy was a man of his time or even a little earlier, since he shared two interests with Gladstone, though the first was rather risky for a Prime Minister. Several nights a week, Topsy traipsed the streets of the West End failing to save fallen women. 'He had a soft heart and a great sense of morality,' John said, 'and couldn't bear to ignore those less fortunate than himself. I remember him coming home late one evening after trying to persuade a prostitute in Piccadilly to mend her ways. She told him to fuck off.' Stung but undaunted by such coarse language, Topsy was tenacious if not terribly successful in his cause.

Despite his devout ancestry he was an avowed atheist; his beliefs lay in a more obscure place. Spiritualism was at its height during the mid to late nineteenth century and devotees included statesmen, military leaders and writers such as Conan Doyle; even the grieving Queen Victoria tried it in a desperate effort to contact her late husband, Prince Albert. Caught between the Bible's increasing implausibility and Darwin's natural selection, the Victorians were eager to make sense of a suddenly uncertain world. Spiritualism provided a cutting-edge alternative and was more reassuring than anything else on offer. Equally important, it cut through the social divide: if a Prime Minister's spirit was free then so was a chimney-sweep's or a housemaid's.

Topsy was a free-thinker and an ardent socialist, whether analysing affairs of state with his well-heeled clients or discussing the latest miners' strike with the man who delivered the coal. He liked to hear both sides of a debate and spiritualism was as political as it was intuitive. The séance may also have assumed an aesthetic influence. Known as table-tilting, it was held in a dimly lit room for a practical as well as atmospheric reason: ectoplasm ignites in what the spiritualists called 'sharp white light' and could prove fatal to the medium. This may explain the ghostly illumination in his portraits: he was painting his subjects in the light of the afterlife. In the company of prostitutes and restless spirits, Topsy's night-time pursuits were doubly subfusc.

Money was always in short supply, and while the children were growing up the family moved home many times in the south-west area of London. They eventually settled in a rented top-floor flat at Emperor's Gate in South Kensington, full of books and half-finished canvases stacked against the walls. Topsy was the breadwinner but it was his wife who was in charge. Diminutive, dainty and invariably dressed in black, Gwendolyn was neatly buttoned-up in Victorian sensibilities, the most apparent of which was shame. Her father was Hamnet Hyde-Clarke, descendant of feudal landlords and slave traders, but it was her mother, Emma Davis, who brought the disgrace: she was illegitimate and her daughter never forgave her for it. Blinkered by her sense of propriety, Gwendolyn was far more wary of her mother's questionable lineage than the centuries of forced labour her father's ancestors had inflicted. This unforgiving streak would later divide her family and incite life-long resentment from her elder son, John.

Emma loved the joys of pregnancy, the alluring glow and impending applause of motherhood, but she didn't like the mucki-ness of looking after babies and passed them on to her mother-in-law within weeks of giving birth. Gwendolyn and her younger sister Eva were brought up by their paternal grandmother in Bath. Her first name is missing from the family tree but as the imperious matriarch she inhabited the title Granny Hyde. It was a sheltered childhood of governesses and tutors. Safeguarding against the potential for social slight caused by their mother's unseemly origins, Granny Hyde rarely allowed her granddaughters to play with other children. Little is known of Hamnet other than that he was an absent father who held a tight grip on the purse-strings.

Gwendolyn and Eva grew up pampered and protected and wanted for nothing, except parental love and affection. Granny Hyde did her best: her girls were sufficiently educated — in other words proficient at the piano, French and German, with dancing lessons attended and table manners polished. Shortly before her eighteenth birthday, Gwendolyn's hair went up and her hemline came down, the code that signified she was ready to enter society. The Hyde-Clarkes had slipped several places down the register, but what hopes Granny Hyde had for Gwendolyn's future were about to be dashed.

Petite and curvaceous with shiny black hair pinned in a chignon, she was dressed in white: a lily-shaped skirt, blouse appliquéd and lace trimmed over what was known as a balcony bust shored up by attendant corsetry, and finished off with kid gloves and a fringed parasol. Subtly symbolic and designed to promote status — white for virtue, flourishes for conspicuous consumption — her day outfit advertised her availability. While out for an afternoon stroll one day, chaperoned by her dotty maiden aunt Frances, Gwendolyn stopped at the Bath Canal. Watching the barges pass, they were approached by a tall young man with an elegant bearing and a hint of brogue to his speech. Having enchanted the ingenuous and inattentive Aunt Frances, he took Gwendolyn aside and delivered a winning pick-up line: 'Would you allow me to paint your portrait?'

At twenty-eight, Topsy was ten years her senior and barely making a living. The Hyde-Clarke girls were supposed to marry up not down and they had no choice but to elope. Gwendolyn was immediately disowned by her father. By then the flighty Emma had run off with a younger man and wouldn't have given two hoots who her daughters ended up with, but Granny Hyde must have been appalled. It was 1901 and elopement was an unspeakable breach of protocol, let alone decorum. Hamnet blamed Granny Hyde who blamed silly, slapdash Frances.

At the turn of the century, the aristocratic marriage was based on a contract of intricate negotiations. As a union of land and capital, money talked and attraction to your betrothed was a bonus not a given. Courtships were lengthy but engagements brief: once prospects had been determined and the dowry dealt with, no time was wasted before proclaiming the banns. The bride-to-be conceded to her elders and betters, always and she did it with modesty and grace. What nerve Gwendolyn had flouting convention and rejecting her birthright. She couldn't have offended her family more if she'd absconded with the gardener.

Gwendolyn left behind the fragrant gentility of flower-arranging in the morning room and a spot of embroidery in the afternoon for the frugality of Topsy's Kensington bed-sit and the reek of turps and oil paint. She had no idea how to cook or even where one bought groceries; at home, luncheon and supper magically appeared at the sound of a gong. Everything she knew about domesticity she learned from Topsy. In their different ways they were unworldly, penniless innocents setting off on a grand adventure.

Belle Époque decadence was in vogue. Opulent and organic, art nouveau was all shimmering peacock feathers and poppies in bloom, foliage entwined and tendrils snaked around Lalique glassware and Tiffany lampshades. The sinuous eroticism of Aubrey Beardsley and the Aesthetic Movement's undressed sensuality were too outré for Topsy who would have blushed at the sight of a bare breast on a scantily clad siren. Titillation was for the likes of Mucha and Klimt; Topsy was of the old school and no iconoclast. However, with a new King and a new outlook Edwardian England was loosening its cultural stays.

Despite her unconventional marriage, Gwendolyn was restrained by more than her whale-boned corset: she was the keeper of what she believed to be a dirty little secret. Emma was a faithless bolter and Hamnet could never be certain of his daughter's paternity. Perhaps this was why he cut her off so callously: he'd given her a name and this was how the ungrateful child repaid him. Either way, the stigma of what was politely termed 'misbegotten' left its mark.

I asked John if he remembered his father painting Gwendolyn. 'Never,' he said. 'She was far too reserved and didn't like to be on show. When you sit for a portrait you're exposed for hours on end and there's nowhere to hide, and my mother felt she had a lot to hide.' As with other aspects of family lore, John was mistaken. My cousin Sheila has a framed charcoal drawing of Gwendolyn signed by Topsy and dated 1901. It's the portrait he requested when they met at the Bath Canal. Pretty with pouty lips and a round face, she looked full of life and laughter. Topsy brought out the best in her, but he was the only person she allowed to see past her customary reserve.

Their first child, Vera, was born in 1905, Pauline six years later and John in 1915. Topsy provided the moral guidance and Gwendolyn the discipline: her children were courteous and their manners impeccable. 'She was a good mother in the sense that she would do anything for us but she couldn't show her affections easily,' Pauline said. 'She didn't like to be touched and I can't recall ever sitting on her lap or hugging her.' John's view was much harsher, and with good reason: 'She was standoffish at best, a Tartar at worst. We were never close, especially after the accident.'

Gwendolyn was forty and Topsy fifty when my father was born in 1923. Vera had left home by now and didn't feature much in my father's early years, but for Pauline he was the golden child who could do no wrong. She was twelve and thought of him as her live baby doll. She changed his nappies and fed him his bottle and as soon as he could talk, he called her Sissy Pauli.

John was eight years older than my father and despite the age difference they were the best of friends when they were children. John loved to make up stories for him about a little boy called Sammy. They stayed up late into the night in the bedroom they shared, co-writing Sammy's adventures. Together they crossed oceans and scaled mountains, fought tigers in the jungle and won desert battles.

It was in this room at the age of five that my father's life took its first wrong turn. After collecting conkers in the park one afternoon, he went looking for a pair of scissors to cut a piece of string when he found John's penknife hidden in a drawer. As he tried to cut the string his fingers slipped, driving the blade into his right eye. Screaming and covered in blood, it was Sissy Pauli he ran to. Pauline picked him up and rushed across the road to the doctor who lived opposite. The doctor drove them to Moorfields Hospital where the injured eye was removed to prevent 'sympathetic opthalmia', blindness in the remaining eye.

John told me the story many times over the years, always ending with the same words:

'I've never forgiven myself.' His mother never forgave him either. When my father came home from the hospital they were forbidden to talk about the accident. Not long after, he came to the breakfast table without his glass eye. 'Mummy was horrified,' Pauline said, 'and told him not to do it again.' After that it was never referred to and he grew up believing it was something to be ashamed of. Both my father and John were sentenced to silence. This was in part due to Topsy's squeamishness, but there may have been a more significant reason: as an artist sight was one of his most valuable assets. In the portrait he later painted of my father his face is turned to the right as if Topsy couldn't bear to look at his son's blind side.

Gwendolyn needed someone to blame but she would pay a great price for it. My father's accident was the unhealed wound that marked John's relationship with his mother. When she died, forty years later, he refused to go to her funeral. Marred by feuds and grudges, funerals are tricky on both sides of my family: we have long memories and past injustices remain unforgiven.

3

Coal Dust and Debris

After I was sent back to my grandparents, shortly before my fifth birthday, my father was persona non grata. I didn't understand why and no one would tell me. On the rare occasions my mother was mentioned she was portrayed in sacred terms — 'God called her', 'only the good die young' or 'heaven's angel she was' — but Grandma's euphemisms only exacerbated my ignorance. The closest she came to revealing a bare fact was when she said, 'Joan was very tired when she died.' She always called her Joan and after a while I felt awkward saying the word 'Mummy', as if it belonged to some other child.

All my memories of my mother are borrowed, but at that age I had no difficulty reaching her in the most tangible of ways. I used to sit on my bed surrounded by the few possessions Grandma had salvaged: a bottle-green jumper so soft it almost purred in my hands, a pearl ring, a watch with an ivory face and a leather strap as thin as a liquorice bootlace and a tiny silver box with her broken rosary inside it.

The most treasured item of all lay wrapped in yellowing newspaper in the top drawer of a bureau in the hallway. Grandma told me that my mother had cut off her long hair in a hasty moment and kept it as a souvenir. It was about a foot in length and the colour of the darkest chestnut of late autumn. If I close my eyes I can still feel it against my cheek, silky soft and scented with lavender. As I held it I asked her if she liked vanilla ice cream better than strawberry, whether she loved horses or ballet and who her best friend was. Beyond such small wonderings, I had few questions, and I couldn't find the words for the simplest and most important. These one-way conversations brought me no answers; my imagination allowed me to picture her but I couldn't hear her. If I could retrieve only one memory, it would be the sound of her voice.

★ ★ ★

A child of the Depression, my mother was born in Merthyr Tydfil in 1931, the second of Alf and Anne's four children. Food was scarce, health precarious and anxiety rife. At its worst, unemployment in Merthyr reached 43 per cent, and in some districts, such as

Dowlais, it was closer to 80 per cent. Coal was still the town's primary resource, though the iron and steelworks, and hence the furnaces, had all but closed by 1918. Production was in rapid decline but at its most prosperous, South Wales provided work for more than 250,000 miners and produced one third of the world's coal exports. By 1929, it had dropped to 3 per cent. Merthyr was losing its identity, but holding on to its industrial past with grim determination.

At the turn of the century my great grandfather, Evan Howells, was a trade union activist fighting for miners' rights alongside Keir Hardie, founder of the Independent Labour Party and Merthyr's MP. From nearby Bedlinog, or 'Little Moscow', Communist Party delegates frequently travelled to Russia in support of the Bolshevik cause. Socialist to the core, Evan remembered a time when women and children laboured beside the men. His mother-in-law, Jane Jones, had worked down the pit until she lost her thumb in an accident and could no longer wield a pickaxe. She was known as 'Jane the Coal'.

Wherever there were mines there were breweries and Merthyr had six. After a twelve-hour shift and a quick bath in the zinc tub in the kitchen, it was down the pub for a few pints and a smoke. Despite their ruined lungs, tobacco and snuff were as much a part of a miner's kit as his Davey lamp and a handful of sugar-lumps for the pit ponies; a remedial pinch of snuff was the only thing that cleared the ponies' nostrils of coal dust. Cigarettes were sold in tens or sixes: ten Gold Flake for three-pence, six Lucky Star for a penny. My grandpa, Alf, started smoking around the time he went down the pit in 1921 at the age of fourteen. Both were a rite of passage and an inevitability, but if your family had connections you didn't stay below ground for long. Within two years, a job was found for Alf on the buses. Evan wanted a better life for his children and saw no disgrace in nepotism.

Alf was one of nine and his siblings' names evoke the heritage he was so proud of: Dai, Beattie, Gwynnie and Cyril, to name a few. He was born in 1907 at home in Primrose Hill, Twynrodyn (pronounced Toyn for short). It was a steep, narrow street of terraced houses with outside privies and, if you were lucky, a water tap in the yard. His mother, Harriet, was of hardy stock, and despite the fact that nearby Aberdare had the highest infant mortality rate in England and Wales — 213 deaths per 1,000 births — all her children were reasonably healthy, rickets

46

and ringworm aside.

She spent much of her day heaving buckets of water from the yard for the never-ending grind of housework. Walls and windows were washed to remove the grimy residue of kerosene lighting, the tiled floors mopped and polished, and no self-respecting housewife left her front step unscrubbed. Children bathed once a week at most, but for husbands and older sons coming home from work coated in coal dust, a bath was a daily necessity; they worked in shifts and the enormous copper pot on the range was rarely off the boil. Laundry was soaked in a solution of soda crystals then scoured with lye soap, leaving hands raw and prone to infection. The drudgery was relentless and many miners' wives died long before their husbands, as was the case with both my great grandmothers. Worn down and worn out, exhaustion was the principal cause of death. In a photograph taken in the early 1920s, Harriet is a picture of fatigue, haggard and bowed, with her gnarled hands resting on her knees. She was about forty-five but could have passed for seventy.

There wasn't much time for childcare. After school, Alf and his brothers and sisters were turfed out of the house with a bottle of home-made ginger beer brewed from stinging nettles. They played in the street or down the Inky, the coal tip at the bottom of Primrose Hill. None of the neighbourhood children owned a bike or even a kite, but if you had a spinning top or a few marbles you considered yourself well-off. The props for their outdoor pursuits were improvised or inventively acquired, and animals and their innards featured in their play-time. When I was little, Grandpa took great delight in telling me about a ball game called 'bat and catty', a variation of rounders played with a stick and an inflated sheep's bladder begged from the abattoir. They tied tin cans to cats' tails and raced, or rather pushed, snails along the flagstones with the spike of their mother's umbrella. 'Happy as Larry we were,' he said.

In 1911 Alf's older brother Tommy was one of the first children in Merthyr to take the 11-plus. He passed with high marks, but that year widespread strikes and riots meant that his father barely made an income and couldn't pay for the uniform for Cyfarthfa Castle Grammar. Alf did equally well at school and was particularly good at maths, but when his turn came to take the 11-plus the First World War was drawing to a close and further education was out of the question: families needed wage-earners not scholars. Three years later the foghorn siren called and down in the cage he went.

You didn't see many tall miners in Wales: the smaller they were the more room there was to manoeuvre. Wiry and tough, what the Howells boys lacked in stature they made up for in stamina. They were also good-looking, with sharply defined cheekbones, strong jawlines and Celtic colouring: Mediterranean-blue eyes and thick dark hair, though Alf started to lose his in his late twenties.

The one exception was Cyril, his youngest brother. Six foot and gangly, he was the misfit and the black sheep and many of the Howells' stories relate to his misfortunes and misdemeanours. Everyone loved Cyril. He was a Walter Mitty, a rogue and a joker, and whatever he was up to he always got away with it. Well, nearly. When his turn came to go down the pit, he couldn't be doing with all that hard work and instead spent his shift playing cards with the old-timers at the pub or daydreaming as he wandered the Beacons. When the cage came up he'd head back to the pithead having rubbed his face and vest with coal dust. It worked for a few weeks but he forgot he'd have to take home his wages. With his gift for guile he no doubt came up with a feasible excuse.

If Cyril had an opposite it was his sister Dolly. She was a pretty girl but, as the Welsh say, one cup short of a tea set. She couldn't grasp irony or idiom and took everything at face value. She also had a compulsion for honesty. When they were teenagers Cyril had a scruffy little mutt called Spot. One day Dolly accidentally locked the dog in her parents' bedroom. Fractious and fed up, Spot ripped up the curtains, the bed-spread and anything else he could get his claws on. Her mother was furious and in a temper shouted at Dolly, 'Get rid of that bloody dog.' She meant put him in the back garden, but it was lost on Dolly who promptly took the unfortunate Spot to the neighbourhood poacher. When Cyril came home from 'work', he asked where the dog was. 'Go and look in the yard,' Dolly said. Leaning against a small mound of earth was a makeshift headstone that read: 'Here lies Spot, who was shot.' It was some years before Cyril saw the funny side.

Judging by her snappy couplet I'd say Dolly was sharper than she was given credit for. Understated and unforced, such wit is the stuff of playwrights and poets, yet it doesn't seem to travel easily; on the English side of the Severn Bridge not many can name a Welsh writer other than Dylan Thomas. *Under Milk Wood* is subtitled 'A Play for Voices', and it's a given that the dialogue needs to be spoken aloud. In tune with the landscape, the Taffy accent rises and falls following a melodious trail along mountains and valleys. Lightning fast and self-mocking, or, like Dolly's epitaph, cruelly concise, the Welsh waste few words. Over lunch recently, my Auntie Marlene said to her cousin Hugh, 'Handsome you are, like Douglas Fairbanks and Errol Flynn.' Right on cue Hugh said, 'Douglas Flynn then, is it?'

Cyril was also a master of the one-liner. He could talk his way out of any amount of trouble and loved to have the last word. Light-fingered and quick on his feet, he was more chancer than felon and had little respect for authority. He was never divorced from his first wife, but with characteristic disregard for the law he remarried anyway. He was charged with bigamy and should have received a sentence. At his trial, he got away with a fine and a thorough telling-off from the judge. As he was escorted from the dock Cyril turned to the bench and delivered his parting shot: 'Says you.'

This frugality with the spoken word also applied to the Celtic sense of self. Like Jane the Coal, you were named for what you did. Jones the Fish or Lloyd the Post needed no explanation, while others played with the patronymic — Billy Twice (William Williams)

51

— or exposed a personal trait, such as Pugh the Few (the miser), Dilys the Plenty (the good-time girl) and best of all, Dai Never Never (the celibate). A similar dubbing was applied to animals. Household rubbish was rarely collected but roaming goats would clear it for free and were called Billy the Bins. As a result of the refuse and a lack of indoor plumbing, infestation was unavoidable. Grandpa told me that his mother kept a hedgehog in the kitchen, but not as a pet. It slept in a cupboard during the day and came out at night to eat the bugs. I asked him if it had a name. 'Bugger All,' he said. It took me a minute to work that one out.

Enclosed within the Taff Valley and scarred by its industrial past, no one could call the town pretty or picturesque, scattered as it was with towering slag heaps, the worthless debris from centuries of excavation. It was hard to see beauty in these morbid carbon copies of the Brecon Beacons, but as Grandpa often said, 'We were living in God's pocket.' Life revolved around work, home and hearth, and there was always coal for the fire at Primrose Hill.

Barring economic necessity, his generation didn't see a need for abroad and he had no desire to travel further than the confines of Tredegar and Treharris. To Grandpa, London was a city as foreign as Paris or New York, but in his mid forties he ended up moving to England's capital. He kept it to himself, but leaving Merthyr broke his heart. His veins ran with Celtic blood and his personality was loded with the iron of pride, stoicism and solitariness, traits he smelted into armour that kept the world and its worries at bay.

Grandpa didn't fight in either of the world wars. He was too young for the first and too old for the second, but as an employee of the Merthyr Council bus company, he wore his uniform with dignity. Forty or so years later, he refused to watch the 1970s TV series *On the Buses*; he was offended by its portrayal of drivers and clippies as dimwits and womanising layabouts. In his day, public transport was the arterial system of the community and the depot its heart. Drivers especially were figures of respect: they got you where you needed to go and on time.

In 1927 Alf married Anne Evans. He was quite a catch, diligent, pensive and as dependable as the bus timetable. Anne was a looker too, with her wavy black hair, flawless complexion and a smile that was one part winsome to two parts wistful, as if she were already resigned to loss and hardship. Her parents and their five children lived in a council house in Bryngoleu, Aberfan, a social

53

cut above Toyn where Alf grew up. Council houses were the inverse of what they are now: you had to be in work to afford the rent. Anne's father, Tom Evans, was a miner and a deacon at the Baptist chapel. With his wife Annie, he was in charge of the entertainment at the local Temperance Hall and stringently vetted it for decency. There were no dancing girls or lewd comedians: Tom was partial to male voice choirs, colliery brass bands and the occasional Eisteddfod-winning poet. They also ran the hall's sweetshop and their nickname was Evans the Mintoes. Behind their backs Alf's family called them Lord and Lady Minto.

Alf's was a childhood of hand-me-downs patched at the knees and elbows, and his father and brothers congregated at the pub rather than the chapel. Anne went to school in smart, clean clothes run up on her mother's treadle-driven Singer. Her father never touched anything stronger than Adam's Ale, as they called the water from a nearby spring. Teetotal and with fewer children to feed, they had a little more money to spend. Annie was an elegant woman, always beautifully turned out beside her sprightly husband in his spruce suit and polished boots. As strict chapel-goers they believed appearances were important; you could say it was the sartorial equivalent of cleanliness is next to godliness. Dressed up in their finery, they walked to chapel three times a day on Sundays. Baptists weren't allowed to ride a bike or even cook on the Sabbath, so there were no roast dinners, only cold leftovers.

The chapel also followed this parsimony in its rejection of Catholicism's opulence: oak pews were uncarved, floors earthen and windows unadorned. Latin had excluded the multitude, but for the Nonconformists faith was expressed in words as opposed to ritual, and in English not Welsh, which had been in sharp decline from the turn of the century. Perhaps more than any other denomination, Baptists put the protest into Protestantism and claimed the pulpit in place of the altar as their focal point. Elevated and enclosed, it was designed to project the voice. Bellowed rather than spoken, sermons were all saints and sinners, repentance and salvation; 'The end is nigh' was one of the most prevalent cautions. Visiting preachers were PR-savvy and idolised like latter-day celebrities. On tour in the provinces these soul-winners, or sky pilots as they were known, played to capacity houses. Warning of calamity and foreboding, hell in the guise of temptation was never far from your front door.

God-fearing and grim-faced, my great

grandparents' framed photographs hung side by side in the hallway of our flat at Hyde Park Gardens, Annie severe in a high-necked lace blouse and Tom with a coal black moustache and an eagle-eyed glare. Having forsaken alcohol, bad language, tobacco and gambling, their only vice was vanity, as though life were to be endured rather than enjoyed.

This was the family my mother was born into: on the one side, hellfire and damnation, on the other borderline Communist atheism. No wonder she didn't know which way to turn.

★ ★ ★

Grandma kept her faith but she wasn't overly pious. She liked the occasional glass of Mackeson's stout and didn't mind Grandpa having a flutter on the Grand National, though she did make me go to Sunday school at the nearest church when I was about six. St John's was Church of England, but for some reason she wasn't fussy about its doctrine. The best part of Sunday school was the Tree Top orange squash and jammy dodgers after prayers, which was either a reward or a bribe. I liked the stories but never really got to grips with the praying. As we knelt in a circle with eyes squeezed shut and hands pressed together, my mind wandered and I had a tendency to hum tunelessly to myself. I was frequently told off for asking the wrong kind of question. The one I remember most vividly was: 'When St Paul wrote all those letters to the Corinthians, did they ever write back?' The teacher said I was facetious, then she made me look it up in the dictionary and read the definition aloud. It was pretty accurate. Not long after the letter-writing question I was asked to leave: apparently I was what they now call disruptive. Excluded from Sunday school, I never returned to the fold.

As a child my mother didn't show much interest in religion either, though she made up for it later. Nor did she have much in common with her parents. She inherited her father's colouring and her mother's nervous disposition, but in most other respects she was a changeling, and a delicate one. Her older brother Howard told me that my mother was terribly ill when she was a baby and almost died. The only thing that cured her was the water from the spring in Aberfan. Adam's Ale may or may not have held healing properties but Grandma believed it saved her daughter's life. When it came to old wives' tales she had her own particular convictions: green melon hastened a cold, raw potatoes cured a stammer and, despite its lurid colouring, Lucozade was nature's antibiotic.

They never found out what was wrong with my mother, but it contributed to Grandma's infatuation with illness, as if she needed the attention that came with having sickly children. Unlike his three siblings, Howard was — and still is at seventy-five — tough and healthy and refused to pander to his mother's hypochondria-by-proxy. 'She couldn't help mollycoddling,' he said, 'but in the long run it did no one any favours.'

Grandma's anxieties stemmed from the 'Hungry Thirties' when one in five children in Merthyr died before their fifth birthday, mostly from diphtheria or malnutrition. It wasn't much better for adults. In 1932 life expectancy was forty-six: the symptoms were deprivation and disease but the cause was unemployment. It was said that 'A man with a job attracted sightseers,' but Grandpa, unlike so many of his neighbours, was never out of work.

'We were luckier than most, but food was still a constant preoccupation because Mum was such a terrible cook,' Howard said. 'There was never much of it, just enough on your plate to leave you wanting more. It wasn't penny-pinching, it was the Baptist belief in 'Waste not, want not.'' It was probably one of the reasons Grandpa slept so much: he was underfed and low on energy. The other reason was strategic: sleep was his shield against Grandma's barrage of chatter.

As the Depression was superseded by the Second World War, Grandpa was promoted from conductor to driver and later inspector. A man of his background had few expectations beyond marriage, children and a two-up two-down. Hopes and dreams didn't feature in his life-plan except for a bit of peace and quiet, not that he got much of it. He was henpecked and it was Grandma who ruled the roost, but he loved his job, in part because it got him out of the house.

Home was a rented house in Mardy Terrace, just outside the town centre. It was stuffed full of furniture of no particular style other than old-fashioned. There wasn't much room to manoeuvre around the drop-leaf table, bentwood chairs and plywood sideboard neatly crammed with mismatched crockery and glassware, all arranged around a Portadyne accumulator wireless weighing in at around forty pounds. Ornaments, or knick-knacks as Grandma called them, were mostly souvenirs from seaside trips to Barry Island or Porthcawl: a milk jug decorated with a red dragon breathing the words 'Cymru am Byth' (Wales For Ever), carved

Welsh love spoons and a plaster paperweight of Cardiff Castle.

The framed photographs of Tom and Annie Evans glared down from their eyrie above the fireplace, warning the children of the perils of extravagance and disobedience. Bad behaviour wasn't normally tolerated but Grandma made excuses for her delicate daughter. Howard and Joan were born sixteen months apart but their mother's affection was unevenly distributed: 'I remember Joan had a tantrum in the middle of Woolworth's and smashed her china doll on the floor. Mum picked up the pieces and didn't say a word, whereas I would have got a clip round the ear.'

In the early 1930s toys were scarce. 'We still had gaslight then,' Howard said, 'and Dad brought home a couple of dead light bulbs from the bus depot for me to play with. That was Dad for you.' In a world of his own, Grandpa thought they were a novelty and therefore a plaything. Who knows what Grandma thought; perhaps that her rebellious, robust little boy was immune to injury since he wouldn't toe the infirmity line, even at that age. My mother was given a china doll, Howard light bulbs: prone to favouritism, once she'd made up her mind Grandma was immovable. Much later, it was the same with me and my cousins.

★ ★ ★

In a photograph of my mother taken in October 1941, her summer freckles are fading and beneath her home-made cardi I can almost see her shoulders shaking with laughter as if she's just delivered the punch line of a joke. She looks like a naughty ten-year-old who would stand up for herself and giggle in the face of adversity. It may have been true at that age but it didn't last long.

Howard's wife Marsli remains as puzzled by my mother now as when they were teenagers and could never really tell what was going on in her head, which was usually buried in a book. Mired in the poetry of legends and quests, my mother kept herself to herself. While her schoolmates played knock-down ginger or taunted the London evacuees, she was at home in her bedroom, daydreaming of castles and a knight on a white horse. Marsli describes her as 'an outsider rather than a misfit. At times there was a remoteness to Joan, as if she'd already left us.' In a way she had, but the disconnection wasn't entirely of her own making.

When she was thirteen, my mother was diagnosed with Sydenham's chorea, or St Vitus' Dance as it was then called. A disease of the nervous system associated with rheumatic fever, its symptoms included fidgeting, involuntary muscular twitches, especially of the face and shoulders, and uncontrollable fits of laughter. At its most severe, chorea can lead to paralysis and loss of speech. Far more common among girls than boys, it was thought to be caused by strep throat and was passed on through coughing and sneezing. My mother spent several months in an isolation ward at a sanatorium. Antibiotics weren't freely available until the late 1940s, and the treatment was long-term bed rest and phenobarbitone, a hypnotic sedative whose barbiturate content was highly addictive. When the doctors said bed rest they meant it: no visitors, no reading, no stimulation of any kind. For a bookish and imaginative girl stuck in bed with nowhere to go but her mind's eye, her daydreams would have assumed an illusory form.

Barbiturates work by depressing brain activity, resulting in an artificial respite from the outside world. Withdrawal brought on seizures, vomiting, delirium and insomnia, and the after-effects can be permanent: like a defective radio, your reception is fuzzy and you're not quite tuned in to the station you want. My mother's dependence on phenobarbitone at such a young age would have lasting consequences.

She eventually recovered and went back to school, subdued, detached and a bit hazy round the edges. Her report from Quaker's Yard Technical Institute for the spring term of 1945 records that she was almost last in her class in maths and third in English, above average in commerce and book-keeping and fair to middling in geography and history. Science didn't feature in the curriculum but shorthand (82 per cent) and typing (64 per cent) were mandatory: Quaker's Yard girls were destined for secretarial posts as opposed to factory work. Judging by her grades and her teachers' comments, at fourteen she was studious but inconsistent.

In May that year the whole country celebrated the end of the war with street parties: children in paper hats wolfed down watery orange juice and flavourless cakes made with powdered eggs and flour so gritty it was said to be one third cattle fodder. Rationing aside, Merthyr got off lightly. Cardiff and Swansea had been heavily bombed, but perhaps the Germans had done their homework and realised that with the closure of the foundries and most of the mines, Merthyr didn't have much worth destroying. The Luftwaffe saved its buzz bombs and doodlebugs for the ports and cities.

Howard and my mother were good friends when they were small, but by the time they reached adolescence they had little common ground. While he was reading *Just William* and *Bulldog Drummond*, she was tackling Tolstoy and Virginia Woolf. Precocious and progressive in certain ways, she was also influenced by ill-fated romanticism. Some of her books now sit on my shelves. Inscribed in blue ink with her name and the year she acquired them, they provide both timeline and insights. I wonder if her life might have turned out differently had her collection featured heroines such as Jane Austen's charmed Emma Woodhouse, rather than the doomed Anna Karenina.

Aside from her love of literature, Howard could only call to mind fleeting impressions of his sister: 'When I think of Joan I always see her smiling. She was a dreamer and a romantic, but it's difficult to say what she was really like.' It's a sentiment I come across frequently, as if her footsteps were so light they barely left a trace. Her cousins also find it difficult to describe her. They all comment on her apparent confidence and composure, but beyond that they struggle to conjure up her picture. One described her as 'different from the rest of us'; another said that she was 'heading places'. Her cousin Hugh had more of a boy's view and the one detail he could recall said more about Grandpa's earnings than my mother's personality: 'Joan was the only one in the street who had a bike.' I couldn't help laugh at that but it also made me wonder where were the anecdotes, the defining characteristics, the remarkable qualities? No one could remember.

Until recently, my image of my mother was based on a handful of photographs. Persuaded by her smile, I wanted to believe she was full of laughter and quick to see the funny side. Marsli, among others, said that my mother was easily hurt and took things far too seriously, as if she were missing several layers of skin. It seems the camera lied and the closer I looked, the more her image dissolved.

After leaving school at sixteen, she temped as a secretary and on Saturdays worked with Marsli as a model and sales assistant at Theo's, Merthyr's smartest dress shop. It was 1947 and clothing would be rationed for another two years. There wasn't much in the way of colour and the outfits she modelled for the town's wealthier matrons were functional rather than flattering. Christian Dior launched his 'New Look' in February that year, but his extravagant, impractical designs — curvaceous bodices and built-in corsetry, and up to twenty-five yards of fabric for a three-quarter-length skirt — would have little impact in Merthyr; the typist, production-line worker and housewife had no use for brocade trimmings or diamanté buttons. The Utility label still governed what passed for fashion and its key word was economy — slim collars, narrow lapels and minimal detail — but even the plainest pencil skirt and tapered jacket, in durable shades of drab, looked elegant on my mother's slender frame. She also made her own clothes, or rather re-fashioned them, the 'make do and mend' necessity of the time. Unpicking the seams of Grandpa's old suit she transformed it into a near-enough designer two-piece, as seen in the pages of *Vogue* or *Harper's Bazaar* — faux couture for the fashion-conscious and hard-up.

At five feet six inches tall, with glossy auburn hair and a smile that opened doors, she was an appealing package. Ahead of her time, she was a prototype woman of the 1950s: sweet-natured and demure, determined and enterprising, but only up to a point. In my mother's day the skills that travelled best were shorthand and typing. With her secretarial facility she could go anywhere and find a job, preferably in a publishing house where her literary ambitions might be encouraged. She fell short, however, on one crucial aspect: thanks to Grandma's mollycoddling she was entirely undomesti-cated.

Marsli often visited the house at Mardy Terrace when she and Howard were courting and was shocked that my mother wasn't even allowed to do the dishes, let alone help with the cooking and housework. Grandma treated her three youngest children like invalids and her cordon sanitaire left them with little resistance to germs. They in turn obliged her with recurring colds and flu, as well as chest and throat infections. For Grandma, the adage 'a bit of dirt never hurt anyone' was blasphemy.

She kept a hankie in her sleeve ready to swipe a smudge or speck of dust and didn't like company messing up the front room. In Merthyr you were judged by how fast you put the kettle on the range. 'Family was family,' my Auntie Olwyn said, 'and we'd stop by everyone's house for a cup of tea and a chat. We'd just knock on the door and walk in, but at Mardy Terrace it was like you were visiting royalty.' Grandma's airs and graces didn't ingratiate her with the Howellses who were more down-to-earth than Evans the Mintoes. Fraternising with the family in Toyn was discouraged and my mother missed out on larking around down the Inky or joshing with her hardier cousins. Garrulous and easy-going, they love a good joke at each other's expense and juggle two or three at a time, landing punch lines left and right. No one takes it personally, but as one of them said, my mother was like an orchid among foxgloves.

By the late 1940s manufacturers such as Kayser Bondor and Berlei, Thorn Electrical and Hoover began to replace the colliery and foundry as the town's chief employers. The industrial landscape slowly healed itself as new factories were built on abandoned mine sites. With near full employment, women left the kitchen for the workplace but it was an interim independence. With marriage rather than a career in mind, many of my mother's contemporaries spent their working lives in the factories, but their real goal remained one of homemaker.

Children who worked and lived at home handed over their weekly wage to their mother, who gave them pocket money. My mother probably received more than most, which she saved for the great escape: London. It would take two years and she used the time productively. Marsli remembers her as diligent and conscientious, whether reorganising the lingerie shelves at Theo's or signing up for overtime at the typing pool.

She liked to keep busy and had an eye for detail and order, but there was a restlessness to her.

This tension may have been a vestige of her bout with Sydenham's chorea and it had few outlets. It didn't surprise me that my mother wasn't sporty, but I'd pictured her kicking up her heels to a local swing band at the union hall. The image deflated when Marsli told me that she and her friends went to sixpenny hops every weekend but my mother would never join them. The knowledge that she didn't dance was one of my most disappointing discoveries; unlike me, I think she was afraid of looking silly on the dance floor. As Marsli said, she didn't know how to let her hair down.

She did, however, know how to reinvent herself. At a finishing school of her own making she took elocution lessons and erased her Welsh accent; on an old upright in the front room she taught herself to play the piano by ear; and, refining her German, she studied the songs of Kurt Weill. From her brief stint as a model she learned to move with economy and grace and how to dress to her best advantage. Poised and polished, she made sure she would fit in anywhere, except Merthyr.

Confined and snug in its valley, the town

was a community united in hardship but satisfied with its lot: you got what you expected and you left disillusionment to those who dared to dream. The family had climbed one or two rungs up from Primrose Hill: they were now well-to-do working class. In her size five court shoes and acquired sophistication, my mother was ready to step over the social divide.

4

Bluecoat Boy

My father wore a paisley-patterned silk cravat, heavy raincoat and big brown shoes scuffed at the heels. Sandy-haired and bearded, he seemed enormous to me but he walked slowly and had trouble keeping up with my small steps. I thought it odd that he wrote with his left hand since everyone else I knew used their right. His shaky italic script crept across the page like an injured spider as he inscribed the books he gave me 'For Anna-Petra'. Until recently he was the only person who called me by my full name.

On alternate Saturdays and Sundays he would collect me from Hyde Park Gardens. Grandma dressed me in my best frock and patent leather Mary-Janes and reluctantly let me go. I didn't have many clothes but she made sure I looked my best. With my hair brushed to a shine and tied back with a bow, she sent me off with: 'That'll show him.' 'Show him what?' I asked. 'Never you mind,' she said. It was one of her most used and most frustrating phrases.

My father didn't take me to the zoo or the funfair. Instead we went to the Royal Opera House, the British Museum or the National Portrait Gallery, his well-intentioned but misguided attempt at my early cultural education. His favourite Sunday morning haunt was Speakers' Corner. I tried to work out what was going on and concluded it was an outdoor theatre for the mad and the furious. Each speaker had to have his own box to stand on and a big voice. They held up pieces of cardboard that said, 'Americans out of Vietnam', 'Free Rhodesia' or 'Food for Biafra'. The crowd would boo and jeer: 'Go back where you came from!' I didn't understand why everyone was so cross or why so many of them had it in for people with dark skin. When they shouted bad words like 'Paki' or 'wog' their faces were twisted and ugly. I thought it was a hateful place. It didn't occur to me then, but at Speakers' Corner my father only stood and listened.

He sometimes forgot I was with him and would leave me in the foyer of the Festival Hall or up in the gods at Sadler's Wells. I was just as heedless and had a tendency to wander off by myself; between the two of us we were a disaster waiting to happen. One day, on the way to Covent Garden we became separated in the crowd. I reached out to hold the hand of a man next to me. The stranger's hand felt safe and when I looked up at him he smiled at the trusting little girl at his side. When my father found me a few minutes later he growled and snatched at my arm. I think he was jealous of the stranger's easy affection.

He was like an angry giant whose smile would turn into a snarl at the least provocation. I remember one particular incident following a visit to the British Museum. The vendors outside were selling balloons and hot dogs. My father bought me a blue balloon and told me to hold on to the ribbon. It was a bright and blustery day and as we stood on the steps of the museum I lost my grip on the ribbon. As I watched my balloon float away he exploded in rage and stamped his foot on the ground. My reaction to these outbursts was always the same: my throat closed and my mind slammed shut — I was struck dumb. At the time I didn't realise why the balloon meant so much to him. Now I understand why he was so angry: he took everything personally and believed everyone was against him, and by losing the balloon so was his daughter.

While my school friends went to see *Bambi* or *Babes in the Wood*, I was taken to Chekhov and Wagner. I longed to go to the panto and shout, 'Oh no he isn't!' and 'Behind you!', but I was stuck with a pair of binoculars and the programme notes for *Tristan and Isolde*. To a six-year-old, costume drama and opera were dreary and endless, and by curtain's fall I was thoroughly grumpy. I dreaded these outings, but for my father culture was sacred and he was appalled that I wasn't getting any of it at home. Looking back, it's obvious he knew his time was running out, but in his rush to educate me his judgement was as shaky as his handwriting.

★　★　★

At around the same age he would have experienced a similarly intellectual environment, but much of it at one step removed. Topsy couldn't afford to take his children to the theatre or the concert hall. Instead, the family gathered round the crystal-set wireless listening to recitals from Wigmore Hall, Shakespeare from the Old Vic and plays by Tyrone Guthrie and Reginald Berkeley. Known as the blind medium, radio influenced my father's view of the world. Through the soundscape of footsteps echoing on an empty street, thunder at midnight or birdsong at daybreak he learned to see the sound and hear the image. When he was about six, his brother John remembers him pointing up at the sky and saying, 'Look at the noise the sun makes.'

In 1929 the news was gloomy and the future bleak. It was the year of the Wall Street Crash, the St Valentine's Day Massacre and a 94 mph hurricane that swept across Britain killing twenty-six people. Having already faced his first crisis, it was a dark year for my father too. After recovering from surgery at Moorfields, his nightly ritual set him apart. While most children said their prayers before going to bed, my father had to remove his glass eye. Every morning he met his loss in the mirror and no one but him saw the empty socket. It was a heavy burden for a little boy to bear alone.

The family was complicit in creating an atmosphere of repressed shame, but they also did their best to make up for it. 'There was a melancholy air about Michael that inspired devotion,' Pauline said, 'but after the accident I think we overdid it. We should have treated him normally, but not being able to talk about his eye made that impossible.' He became the focus of attention, pampered by his mother and sister and indulged by his father. Topsy often took him to the V&A, within walking distance of their flat at

Emperor's Gate. My father's extensive knowledge of art and design originated with a teacher of infinite patience and practical experience.

Topsy was no longer painting by gaslight. Clean, efficient and apparently inexhaustible, electricity transformed life at home, but above all for women. With the introduction of the hire purchase scheme, labour-saving appliances were suddenly affordable. Gwendolyn exchanged her flat-iron for a plug-in and her collection of brushes for a new-fangled Hoover. Her domestic load was also lightened by a maid who doubled as a nanny for my father. 'My parents took pity on a local girl who had lost her job,' Pauline said. 'They gave her room and board and she was paid about five shillings a week, but Mummy often had to borrow it back.'

Poverty for the down-at-heel in South Kensington was terribly civilised. When the bailiff came to tea, as he frequently did, he and Topsy sat at the kitchen table and discussed how the Swans might rearrange their finances. Somehow they did and managed to send the three eldest children to private schools. Vera and Pauline went to Godolphin and Latymer and John to Latymer Upper, but they were sometimes sent home with a note reminding Topsy that the fees hadn't been paid. When it was my father's turn, in 1933, the family was flat broke and Topsy had to find an alternative.

★   ★   ★

Christ's Hospital was founded in 1552 by Edward VI as a home for the City of London's waifs and strays. It's still a charitable foundation and a public school of a different kind. Parents or guardians contribute according to their means; currently around 40 per cent pay nothing at all and only 3 per cent pay full fees. In my father's day, and in mine (1971-7), there were no rich kids at Christ's Hospital. Most of us came from broken homes or were children of the clergy, disabled servicemen or artistic families in financial need. We may not have appreciated it at the time but despite our backgrounds we were fortunate.

The girls moved from Newgate Street in the City to Hertford in 1784 and the boys to Horsham in 1902. The school was backward-looking only in its uniform and the boys' hasn't changed since Tudor times: ankle-length, navy blue woollen coat with silver buttons down the front, collarless white shirt with clerical bands, breeches and bright yellow knee-socks. En masse it looks as if they've stepped out of a sixteenth-century etching.

Soon after its founding the school became known for its rigorous education and went on to produce a disproportionate number of writers, including Samuel Richardson, Samuel Taylor Coleridge, Charles Lamb and John Leigh Hunt. Old Blues also distinguished themselves in other fields: Augustus Pugin in architecture, Constant Lambert in music and Barnes Wallis, inventor of the bouncing bomb. Regardless of their humble beginnings, they were expected to excel.

My father was at Housey, as the boys' school is nicknamed, from 1933 to 1939. Over long conversations with several of his friends I discovered he developed his multifaceted personality early. John Mayes remembers the buzz of excitement in the dorm when they heard that a new boy had a glass eye. At night my father kept it in a glass of water on the locker beside his bed and was quite gleeful at the polite horror it caused as it stared back at anyone peering down at it. For the first time his disability gave him a certain cachet, but he didn't let on in his letters to the family. In one, written during his first term, he warned: 'Nobody knows the misery I am suffering. If you don't take me away from here, it will be the end.' It seemed he played the wounded card at home and claimed to loathe everything about Housey.

His contemporaries remember it differently and describe him as plucky, self-possessed and outspoken. A keen member of the debating society, he preferred to fight for the least popular cause. Like Topsy, he loved a good argument, especially in divinity class, though he admitted a mild regret to Michael Gribble when they were about twelve: 'The trouble with being an atheist is that when something goes right there's no one to say thank you to.' My father had a lot to be thankful for. He already knew where he was heading and was an assiduous scholar when it came to the humanities. The sciences held no interest for him and he did just enough work to pass his exams. He also had little respect for the Housey obsession with hierarchy. While most boys did their best to align themselves with one faction or another, he felt no need to fit in and acquired a reputation as a rebel.

His friends found him inquisitive and quick-witted, though his caustic humour sometimes cut a little close. It also outfoxed the bullies. As one friend said: 'He knew how to buff up a putdown.' Physical intimidation was endemic, from 'fotching' (a whip-crack smack to the head with an open hand) and 'blacking' (boot polish applied to a bare bottom) to holding a boy by his ankles from a third floor dormitory window. The school tyrants earned my father's disdain as much for their lack of imagination as their cowardice, but he knew how to disarm them: along with his verbal dexterity he could shoot a withering look as sharp as an arrow. The bullies weren't smart enough to know what to make of him, so they left him alone and went for the easy targets.

Team sports occupied a major part of life at Housey, but other than cross-country runs and gym he was exempt from PE; with his monoscopic forward vision he couldn't judge the speed and angle of a ball in motion. It was no loss on his part since he had a lot more free time to spend in the library. He also made a benefit out of a handicap: from the safer side of the rugger pitch and the cricket green he learned that the spectator sees more of the game than the players.

The sixteen Houses were named after Old Blues and my father was in Coleridge A. Long after he left school, he attended a dinner at the Reform Club, chaired by Sir William Hamilton Fyfe, former headmaster, in honour of *The Christ's Hospital Book*, a commemoration of the school's 400-year history. The sixty-five contributors were all old boys, who Fyfe called his 'inky Blues'. My father's article links a literary influence with his indifference to sports. He writes that had he been educated elsewhere he might not have felt such a personal connection to Coleridge, having 'the first syllable of his name, followed by the number 18, stitched to my school underwear . . . and stood on a touchline and feebly urged on the house fifteen with the cry of his name'. He ends with: 'I have scraped up an acquaintance in recent years with Henry James, but it has not come with such ease and intimacy as my acquaintance with S.T.C., for I have never worn James' name next to my skin and never bawled his name from a muddy touchline.' Coleridge claims the intimacy, but my father's adulation for the novelist would recur in his writing like a talisman, or rather a tentative unweaving of the literary riddle James set in 1896 — the ambiguous 'figure in the carpet'.

Many of my father's friends have commented on his handsome profile and that he often presented his face at an angle. Necessity rather than vanity caused him to turn his head slightly to the right; it compensated for his blind side but also suggested that he watched and listened with absolute attention. Topsy's portrait of my father from the late

1930s shows him in semi-profile as a skinny-malink with tensed shoulders and a sombre countenance. It would take a few years for the rest of his face to catch up with his patrician nose and cheekbones, but Topsy captured an awkward and edgy teenager who looks as though he'd rather be lying on his bed reading *Punch* or the latest Penguin paperback.

The painting was never framed but Topsy must have liked it, since he usually painted over family portraits when he was short of money and needed a canvas for a paying client. As the custodian of his father's few surviving works, Uncle John gave it to me about twenty years ago. Every now and then I think about taking it to the framers but it's still wrapped in a blanket at the back of my wardrobe. There's something about the grave expression that I find unsettling. My father didn't care for it either; perhaps he felt it was too true a likeness. Even as a teenager he didn't like to give away much about himself.

He preferred to let others do the talking and was an instinctive participant of Mass-Observation, the social research organisation established in 1937. Its name suggests the instrument of a totalitarian state but M-O was no more sinister than a nationwide study of the everyday lives of ordinary people. Its founders called it an 'anthropology of ourselves' and its observers were volunteers of all ages and backgrounds. Today's equivalent might well be reality television, though M-O's findings were no doubt more credible.

Interviewing his school friends and writing M-O reports contributed as much to my father's future career as any of his studies at Housey. 'Michael was inquisitive without being pushy,' Tony Tighe told me, 'and he wasn't afraid of silence. He already had the confidence to know that the pause was merely a breathing space between information.' It was no surprise to his friends that he went on to be a collector of other people's stories.

'At school your father had two party tricks,' Tony said. 'With a pen in each hand he would write out a verse of poetry or a limerick. The script was almost identical.' At the time, the second was far more valuable: 'We were studying in the library one afternoon when he asked me to take any book from the shelf and open it at random. He scanned a page and gave the book back to me, then recited it. After only one reading he was word perfect.' His photographic memory gave him an advantage in exams but while the handwriting trick seemed a mere diversion, the fact that he was ambidextrous took on a far greater significance in later life.

Set in 1,000 acres with its own railway station, farm and fishing pond, Housey looked more like a sprawling country estate than a school. The architect went all out on grandiose, Gothic flourishes on the show buildings such as the chapel, Library and Big School, but penny-pinched on the lodging quarters. Behind the redbrick façades they were almost as spartan as Dickens' Dotheboys Hall, as one of my father's friends said. The boys slept on the old beds from Newgate Street with a straw-filled pillow and one blanket. Those whose family could spare it brought a second blanket from home, others shivered under their bluecoats.

The day began with one of the school's most peculiar rituals. When the bell rang at 7 a.m., the boys lined up beside their beds and on the monitor's order, 'Handkerchiefs out!', blew their noses in ascending house number until they heard him shout, 'Handkerchiefs away!' Nasal drill continued until the 1960s, when the school doctor realised it was a major cause rather than a prevention of cold and flu epidemics.

As disciplined as a military academy, three times a day the seventy-piece band led the boys in marching ranks into the dining hall. Meals were paltry and often inedible, suet and gristle being the cook's principal ingredients. Much of Housey slang was food-related and 'gag' (cold boiled beef), 'dead baby' (jam roly-poly) and 'kiff' (tea or coffee drunk from a bowl) are still in use today. 'Crug' (bread) was spread with jam bought from the tuck shop, where the boys were allowed to spend one shilling a week.

Personal hygiene wasn't a priority and juniors were allocated one bath a week. They were grubby little tykes and Coleridge A's housemaster, C. Blamire Brown, never let them forget it. The least popular of all the masters, even among the staff, Blam was a bitter and disappointed bachelor and a lacklustre Latin teacher. My father's friends described Blam as a soulless ogre, desiccated and totally incompetent. A Magdalen classics scholar, he arrived at Housey in 1912. Twenty or so years later, what little academic inspiration he might have passed on had long dried up and he was allowed to teach only the lowest streams. The best anyone had to say about him was that he had standards: he expected his charges to fall in line with his strict house rules and was outraged when they didn't. He neither liked nor understood children and particularly disapproved of intellectual mavericks, or smart alecks as he called them.

My father exerting his individuality irritated him no end. Blam thought him insolent and frequently told him he was too clever by half. My father always replied, 'Delighted you noticed, sir,' a response that left Blam flummoxed. One of their many run-ins ended with Blam fuming with humiliation. The thinly stocked bookcase in his study included titles such as *King Solomon's Mines*, *Captains Courageous* and the *Biggles* series, *Boy's Own* adventures my father had outgrown. With mock helpfulness, he offered to draw up a reading list for Blam, but was given detention instead.

Only with hindsight did the boys see how sad and friendless Blam was. Miserably miscast in the role of schoolmaster, he was more dutiful masochist than sadist. For some of his colleagues, however, corporal punishment was a perk of the job. 'Luckily for us, Blam didn't have the backbone for it,' Tony Tighe said, 'but other masters were brutal. One in particular initiated his beatings with the command: 'Study the pattern of the carpet, boy!'' The worst offenders were Leslie Waddams and Derrick Macnutt, for whom the cane was the first rather than last resort: the merest hint of the three 'i's — impertinence, insubordination or inadequate work — merited a thrashing. A rebel only when it suited him, my father was adept at avoiding unnecessary punishment; in Waddams' maths class he kept his mouth shut, feigned respect and delivered passable homework on time.

Housey promoted a rigid social structure and boys were accused of 'pansying' if they associated with anyone outside their own house. Left to muddle their way through puberty, few of the juniors knew what it meant since sex education was mostly guesswork. The divide and conquer mentality was designed to discourage what the headmaster, 'Oily' Flecker, referred to as 'sentimental friendships' or 'mutual arrangements'. It didn't work. If discovered, homosexuality led to immediate expulsion, but only in certain cases. Flecker made concessions for brainy boys heading for university. Academic results and reflected glory came before integrity and it was the less gifted who were sent home in disgrace.

Tony Tighe estimated that around 60 per cent of the school was active in one way or another. He said there was a lot of covert sexual experimentation in the dorms, but my father was again the odd one out and never a part of it. John Mayes agrees: 'Michael was always talking about girls and couldn't understand boys being interested in each other like that. In fact he was quite scornful of it.' His attitude changed soon after he left

Housey when he realised a little ambiguity might well help his career.

Of all the Housey masters, the one who stood out for his belief that teaching was a vocation and a privilege was David Stowell Roberts, head of history. The juniors called him Daddy Roberts, the older boys D.S.R. The tough trio of Waddams, Macnutt and Flecker thought him soft but envied the adulation he inspired. Renowned as a talent-spotter, he singled out and nurtured exceptional pupils and encouraged them to think for themselves, a subversive approach in a school run on discipline and observance. His students still remember two of his most constructive edicts: 'Listen for the ring in the sentence,' and 'Either master or avoid the metaphor.' An art collector and amateur painter, he also introduced them to the visual arts, including architecture. D.S.R.'s influence on my father lasted well beyond school and is evident in all his books but one.

During their limited free time, while his friends were caught up in the rough and tumble of rugby fives or earning Boy Scout badges, my father's mind was on higher things. Aside from the library, my father's favourite hideout was the chemistry lab which housed one of the school's few radios. He'd lie on his back on a bench listening to the

Home Service broadcasts from the Albert Hall. He was drawn to the German composers but most of all to Wagner. It was the beginning of a lifelong love-hate fascination: in trying to figure out how such an ugly human being could create such beautiful music, he discovered a paradox that would become a recurring theme in his later writing. He also borrowed a one-line signature tune from *Lohengrin*'s swan prince, which he sang in an exaggerated baritone: '*Ich bin ein Schwan.*'

My father's friends thought him sophisticated beyond his years. 'He was always more mature and street-wise than we were,' Michael Gribble said. 'I had the impression he knew more about chorus girls, women and sex, and the harsher ways of the world than the rest of us.' Conversation around the dinner table at home covered politics, the arts and current events: the Swans were a family who talked to each other, as long as the subject was above board. My father acquired his maturity vicariously from his older siblings. His brother John was studying medicine at the Middlesex Hospital and his stories were now far more riveting than Sammy's desert and jungle escapades. 'Michael was full of questions,' John said. 'Among other things, he wanted to know what it was like to kiss a girl and how one might persuade her into bed.' John, being an outrageous flirt, had most of the answers. Unsurprisingly, Topsy's 'hanky-panky' caution had no impact on either of his sons.

My father's oldest sister Vera provoked the most curiosity, even in absence. Of all the children, she was the most audacious, as well as the naughtiest. John said she was frightfully misbehaved and inconsiderate, staying out until dawn drinking cocktails and dancing in nightclubs with her racy theatre friends. Gwendolyn, formidable as she was, had no control over her wayward, profligate daughter, and even mild-mannered Topsy lost his temper with her. Nearly fifty years later, my white-haired and twinkly auntie would give me a box of Quality Street with the whispered caveat: '*Do* eat them all at once.'

At the beginning of the Roaring Twenties, with minimal formal training, Vera became a dancer after she saw an advertisement for an open audition in *Dancing Times* placed by the Indian choreographer Uday Shankar, Ravi's older brother. Vera was well practised in the fast-paced shimmy, quickstep and bunny-hug, and had no trouble adapting to the complicated and codified discipline of the temple dancer. At that time even ballet was still considered a mildly disreputable profession but it was unheard of for an eighteen-year-old white girl to dance Bharata Natyam and Kathakali. In her bejewelled, flimsy costumes, with a *bindi* slightly misplaced, Vera made the most of her acquired skills — one of her specialities was the infamous, to say nothing of fraudulent, Indian Rope Trick.

Now credited as the founder of modern Indian dance, Uday Shankar became an overnight star in 1923 when he and his troupe performed at Covent Garden with Anna Pavlova in two works he created for her. Vera's moment of glory was her sole performance as the Bride in *Hindu Wedding*, during which she upstaged Pavlova's Beggar Girl. When the curtain came down on the opening night the prima ballerina insisted they switch roles. Following rave reviews, Uday and his dancers joined Pavlova's company for a twenty-nine-date tour of the States, Vera in rags as Pavlova inhabited her exquisite bridal sari.

When they came back to London, Vera and Uday briefly lived together. Had they known, Topsy and Gwendolyn would have been appalled, not least by the short-lived engagement; apparently hyprocrisy had its limits. She took after her parents in one respect only: she married in secret not long after returning to Emperor's Gate. Pauline remembers Vera coming home in the early hours one morning. Topsy barged into their bedroom demanding to know where she'd been. 'I've just got married,' Vera answered, 'and his name is Sidari Lall.' Topsy was aghast and said, 'You've married an *Indian*?' He wasn't quite as broad-minded as he thought.

By the time my father was at Housey, Vera had left the stage and moved to Delhi with her husband and two young daughters. Despite his reticence I doubt her youngest brother could resist such opening lines as: 'When my sister danced with Pavlova . . . ' or 'Did I tell you about my nieces in Delhi?'

My father's six years at Housey were a mix of achievement and forbearance. Aside from Blam, his only other adversary was Keith Douglas, who would soon be remembered as one of the finest poets of the Second World War. In a school where conformity and obedience were the norm, both were confrontational and obstinate. Douglas was an athlete with a taste for jazz, a gun enthusiast and a fanatical member of the Officer Training Corps, my father an aesthete, pacifist and a disciple of classical music. Yet they were more alike than either would have admitted at the time. As well as winning prizes in English and history, they had at least three things in common: poor eyesight, a promising literary career and memorable middle names — Douglas' was Castellain and my father's Lancelot, the lover of Queen Guinevere. My father's role as romantic rival began in 1938 when he and Douglas both fell for a local girl named Liz Brodie whose family owned a farm not far from Housey. Fair-haired and fresh-faced, she was the kind of girl boys fight over.

Douglas was seventeen and my father fifteen, and both exhibited a self-confidence that wasn't quite as genuine as it appeared. Each had his physical inadequacy, in Douglas' case beady eyes and an enormous nose; as he said himself, 'I have the face of a parrot.' It's not clear whether Liz ever made up her mind who she liked best. 'She and Douglas shared a love of horses,' John Mayes said, 'but your father was much better-looking and more gracious. It was a case of 'what does she see in that oaf?'' He was amused and a little envious of the poems Douglas wrote for Liz, a few of which were published in the school magazine, the *Outlook*. For my father, however, the relationship was little more than fond feelings heightened by the dynamics of a teenage love triangle.

John went on to recall a potentially dangerous incident that reinforced my father's dislike of Douglas. One Sunday afternoon John and my father were walking in the direction of the Brodie farm when they ran into Douglas and two of his friends on horseback. 'Suddenly they began cantering around us. They were only showing off but your father couldn't judge distances properly and found it far more threatening than I did. He spoke scathingly of Douglas after that, saying it was all apiece with his absurd militarist fantasies and obsessions.'

My father may have been obstinate but he was always open to a change of opinion. Towards the end of the war he was an editor at Nicholson and Watson, who published Douglas' *Selected Poems* and his only prose work, *Alamein to Zem Zem*. When it came to the printed page, the schoolboy hostility evaporated. My father admired his writing enormously and regretted he hadn't taken him more seriously at Housey. I imagine he would have been struck by one particular line in an early poem, 'How easy it is to make a ghost.' Keith Douglas was killed on the third day of the Normandy landings, aged twenty-four.

My father's friends went on to follow a

variety of professions including pathologist, academic, physicist, farmer, military commander and actor. Most have mixed feelings about Housey, but I think my father might have reluctantly admitted that the element he most disliked, discipline, turned out to be one of his greatest assets.

All but one of his friends were surprised he didn't stay on as a Grecian (sixth-form university candidate). 'Michael believed hands-on experience would give him far more of an advantage than a tertiary education,' John Mayes said. 'Thanks to D.S.R. he didn't need to be told what to think, and had no desire to conform to yet another arid and dying set of cultural values.' Along with a photographic memory, he already had a fertile mind and felt academia might stifle his potential.

By the age of sixteen he'd had enough of the cumbersome bluecoat and all it represented. After passing the School Certificate, he left Housey and was apprenticed to an advertising agency, Saward, Baker and Co. on Chancery Lane, a sideways step towards publishing. My father would prove wrong E.M. Forster's proclamation: '1939 was not a year in which to start a literary career.'

5

Nomad's Land

On New Year's Eve 1967, two weeks after my seventh birthday, I was sitting on the floor of my bedroom drawing a picture of a pony. Lost in thoughts of gymkhanas and blue rosettes I didn't notice Grandma come into the room. When she told me my father had died of pneumonia, I looked up and said, 'Does that mean I won't have to go to the opera any more?' She nodded: 'Best not tell anyone at school, they wouldn't understand.' 'Understand what?' I asked, but she didn't answer. I put the news away and went back to my drawing. I was good at putting things away. My room was neat and tidy, my toys stacked on shelves and my two teddies lined up on my bed. I'd learned that from Grandma, along with 'Least said, soonest mended.' My father's death was never mentioned again. Aside from the occasional memory flitting across my mind, I didn't really think about him until my late twenties when I found out he hadn't died of pneumonia.

Children are more pragmatic than they're given credit for. We're born with a box of tricks, and if we're lucky we figure out which ones to use and when. The most effective of all was the emotional vanishing act: I snapped my fingers and disappeared. It wasn't until I came back years later that I realised these tricks don't work for adults.

Stepping back into my bedroom on the morning of New Year's Eve 1967 I've tried to retrieve the emotions I ought to have felt having just been told my father was dead. There was only one: relief. He deserved more than that but I found no sense of loss, no tears, no grieving. Nor can I remember the last time I saw him. A couple of weeks later I went back to school as if nothing had happened other than Christmas.

Hampden Gurney Primary School was off the Edgware Road, near the Playboy Casino. Seedy and swanky, with a pawnbroker opposite Bechstein Pianos, Woolworth's a few doors down from a chandelier showroom and the cobbler next to the fancy jeweller, it was a tat and tiara neighbourhood. Walking past Lebanese, Indian and Italian restaurants, a Jewish deli and Chinese grocer, my pace slowed as I breathed in the spicy-sweet scent of garlic, coriander and cumin and the exotic accents that accompanied it. Alive with the sounds and smells of foreign lands, I thought the whole world lived on our stretch of the Edgware Road.

My class was made up of a mix of surnames: Patel, Facci, Goldstein, Shevket, Byrne and Hardacre. Johnny Hardacre was the angriest boy in the playground. Sturdily built with a don't-mess-with-me glint in his eye, he was smaller than the other boys but twice as tough. His emotions were close to the surface and he had no trouble expressing them, more often than not with his fists and a two-word expletive. I can't say I liked him, especially after he kicked me in the shins for no reason, but there was something oddly admirable about Johnny. He was upfront and fearless, while I was now guarded and withdrawn. My father's death brought with it a new secret — and secrets meant silence. I was no longer a cheeky little chatterbox.

When I went for tea at my friends' houses, their mothers sometimes asked, 'What do your parents do?' I soon began to dread the question. It made me feel as though I were about to commit an appalling faux pas, but because it was asked by a grown-up I felt I had to tell the truth. My answer invariably brought an awkward response and a swift offer of more cake. There isn't much you can do when confronted with a parentless seven-year-old, other than hold your own children more tightly.

I wonder how my mother would have responded in the same situation. I'd like to think she would have picked that child up in her arms and squeezed her close until it hurt, stroked her hair and cried big, hot tears on her shoulder. When I looked closer at this illusive picture I realised the woman cuddling the seven-year-old is me. I've had to take my mother's place because she wasn't there to watch over me. In one respect it was easy, we could be identical twins and I still see her every time I look in the mirror, but in other ways I felt like a yearling left to fend for itself. I didn't starve or fail to find shelter, and though I managed to defend myself against the bigger beasts roaming my particular savannah I never really felt safe. Grandma did her best but the older I became the harder it was to admit that there were times when only a mother's love and protection will do.

As a child I wanted to be just like my mother; now I want the similarity to end in the mirror. The image I grew up with feels like a counterfeit and I'm struggling to find its original. My research revealed far more than I hoped for but it had a finite life. It couldn't tell me whether she preferred toast or Weetabix in the morning, who she turned to in a crisis or what kept her awake at night; with so many gaps in the story there are moments when I have to make her up as I go along. Whichever way I look at it, my mother left a lacuna that can never be filled.

★   ★   ★

When my mother left Merthyr for London at eighteen, she'd probably never travelled further than Carmarthen or Monmouth. It was a momentous move at such a young age. It took courage to say goodbye to the relative comforts of home and leave behind the friendly and familiar for the anonymity of the big city. To a small-town girl, London must have been overwhelming, from the scale of its museums and monuments to its double-decker buses and Underground travel.

The air was gritty with soot and the buildings black with it. When the smog came down it fell to a soundtrack of coughs and splutters. Bombsites were playgrounds and flimsy prefabs passed for housing. In response to the wartime slogan 'Dig for Victory' gardens remained allotments growing spindly runner beans and sickly broccoli. Below ground, Anderson shelters were refitted for a different kind of refuge. In 1949 the brief period of security was brought to an abrupt end with the start of the Cold War. After Russia tested its first nuclear bomb that year, according to the propaganda, death was once again a part of everyday life. Annihilation was imminent, and few found it easy to see beyond tomorrow, let alone into a long-term future.

My mother lived in Earl's Court. It was renamed the poor man's Chelsea after many of the imposing family homes in the colonnaded crescents and squares were converted into bed-sits during the post-war housing shortage. Behind grandiose front doors, elderly Knightsbridge widows in reduced circumstances shared a kitchen and bathroom with neatly dressed young secretaries and impecunious actors and artists. On the Earl's Court Road, the tea shop, the haberdashery and the pub stood side by side.

Drawn by low rents and short-term lets, the Antipodean connection began during the war; the American GIs commandeered the West End, the Australian servicemen SW5. Nicknamed Kangaroo Valley in the late 1940s, it was the only place in London where you could get an ice-cold beer. For many, including my mother, Earl's Court was a lively layover with abroad in its sights.

Secretarial work suited her for the time being, but Marsli said she flitted from job to job during her first two years in London and was always looking for something better. Among various posts, she worked at the American Embassy in Grosvenor Square. British youth was beginning to fall for all things transatlantic; compared with meagre rations measured by the ounce, even America's cuisine was exotic and sophisticated. The embassy canteen offered delicacies such as milkshakes and hamburgers, with fries instead of chips, and Hershey Bars and Reeses Pieces. For my mother there was always a more desirable job around the next bend and after a few months at the embassy she moved on. At a time when most people were happy to settle for stability and a regular wage, it sounds as if she were in search of the ideal. With it came a seepage of dissatisfaction and an erratic CV, which must have made it difficult to form friendships with co-workers.

In cosmopolitan Earl's Court, background counted for little; my mother was well read, adequately educated and with no discernible accent would have passed for a doctor's daughter from the Home Counties. Everyone was skint but her bohemian neighbours often clubbed together for a bottle-party. The atmosphere was dense with smoke and the scratchy needle of a gramophone played 78s as sculptors and song-writers, playwrights and philosophy students shared the bootleg spoils. I wonder what they made of the shy, smiling girl standing to one side, too inhibited to join in the mambo or the rumba.

My mother may not have danced but she had a passion for music, though I doubt she cared for Perry Como's semi-skimmed ballads or Mantovani's lightweight arrangements. In tune with the period, the bebop and blues revival tapped into the cheerless austerity of the post-war years. It also held up two fingers at the polished commercialism of big-band swing; war-time relics such as 'Moonlight Serenade' and 'Little Brown Jug' were old hat. London had its makeshift equivalents of the Blue Note and the Village Vanguard, such as the Club Eleven on Great Windmill Street, admission half-a-crown, where my mother heard musicians such as Ronnie Scott, Humphrey Lyttelton and George Melly.

She had a soft spot for the tragic heroine, but there wasn't much room for women on the British jazz stage. It was the songs of Edith Piaf and Billie Holiday that most captured her imagination. Prey for heartless lovers and addicted to despair as much as they were to drugs, the Little Sparrow and

Lady Day sang of loneliness and sorrow stripped bare.

When I'd stroked my mother's bottle-green jumper and wrapped her broken rosary around my fingers I'd wondered who her best friend was, but it didn't occur to me she might not have had one. I now recognise this absence of intimate friendships as a familial defect; thankfully, I take after my father. My grandparents lived in London for almost thirty years but the only visitors I remember were relatives from Merthyr and the nanny who lived next door. Of my mother's few friends I've managed to trace, none was a confidante. As one of them said, in the post-war years there was an implicit under-standing that you kept your problems to yourself and never wore your heart on your sleeve.

For my friends and me at eighteen, boys were the main topic of conversation. We wanted to know who got off with who at which party, dissected crushes in minute detail and judged each other by who was on the Pill and who wasn't. Virginity was a hindrance and most of us had given it away for free by then. For someone of my mother's generation and background, girl-talk was anything but candid. If they discussed boyfriends at all it was in terms of a future engagement, alluding to the honeymoon but avoiding its more delicate aspects, while comparing Butterick and McCall's wedding dress patterns. Preoccupied with romance rather than sex, they were nice girls with no need for birth control since virtue was their most treasured asset.

On the one hand, my mother was reticent and evasive, on the other wilful and impulsive. In her love life vigilance took second place. According to Marsli she was very intense with men, 'Joan was always rushing into relationships and ending up heart-broken. She didn't stop still long enough to think things through.' One of my mother's first boyfriends in London was a barrister named Manivel Moodley. Grandma would have referred to him as 'a coloured gentleman', Grandpa that he was as 'black as the ace of spades'.

Mani was a South African-born Indian, big-hearted and jolly, with a smile as dazzling as my mother's. They made a striking couple and everyone in the family liked him. My mother came home one day and said they wanted to get married, but Grandma wouldn't hear of it. At the time, mixed marriages were beyond the bounds of working class respectability; people would talk, and that was one thing she couldn't bear. Years later she admitted to Marsli that she regretted her interfering and that my mother would have been better off with Mani. After my mother died, he stayed in touch with the family, and in an act of tremendous generosity, represented my grandparents at the custody trial brought by my father.

My mother was rarely without a boyfriend, but they were on short-term probation: when the hoped-for proposal was unforthcoming, she moved on. Like her jobs, her boyfriends lasted a few months at most, her expectations dashed before they'd had a chance to develop. When Howard and Marsli were engaged, she asked Marsli, 'How do you get a man to marry you?' My mother was only nineteen but she was in a hurry: wherever she was heading, she needed to get there fast. It's evident in her swiftly scrawled handwriting, her pen barely touching the page, as if she were racing against time.

At home in Merthyr Grandma had taken charge of the domestic chores. Living on her own my mother probably survived on Spam and Bovril sandwiches and cocoa, or occasionally ate out at a Lyons Corner House — sausage and mash 6d, Bakewell tart 2d. There was only one launderette in London, in Bayswater, so she had to wash her clothes in the sink of a shared bathroom. After two years chasing elusive dreams and fending for herself in a poky bed-sit, the capital's appeal was wearing thin.

I never really understood why my grandparents moved to London, nor my mother's part in it, but it set in motion a series of misfortunes, each more disastrous than the last. It was an unhappy family long before leaving Merthyr, but as one of my aunties told me recently: 'Crossing the River Severn was like a curse. Nothing went right for them after that.'

By 1951 Grandpa was an inspector for the Merthyr Council bus company and they owned their own home, in Cromwell Street in the town centre. Behind the net curtains it was a house divided; Grandma's love was strictly conditional, and you had to be on her side. Howard, if not exactly Grandpa's ally, did his best to remain neutral. He left home as soon as he could, at sixteen, and joined the army just after the war ended. My mother and the two youngest, 'Gomez' and Susan, were firmly in their mother's camp.

Grandpa wasn't without his faults as a father, including a short temper. He loved playing with his children when they were little but lost interest once they started talking. A man of few words and absent in both senses, he worked overtime whenever he could, but even when he was home he wasn't entirely present. His faraway gaze carried him to a happier place; I'd like to think he was reliving his childhood, back in the classroom figuring out a complicated mathematical equation or playing 'bat and catty' on Primrose Hill. At Cromwell Street, he was in and out of the dog house for trifling offences, such as a careless slip at a family wedding: he forgot to take Grandma's arm as they made their way to the front of the chapel. She took it as a snub and didn't speak to him for weeks, but I don't think she realised he preferred it that way.

Of all the family stories the following is among the most sketchy yet symbolic, containing as it does more omission than information. In 1951 Grandma went to visit my mother in Earl's Court. A week later she went back to Merthyr and announced that the family was moving to London to run a B&B. It was a hare-brained idea from the start since she couldn't cook and didn't like guests. Grandpa wanted to stay put, but Grandma and my mother presented a united front. In the end he gave in; anything for a quiet life. They packed up their furniture and invested everything in a big house in Streatham. My mother organised the finances through friends of friends who were allegedly property developers. Inexperienced and trusting, she either ignored or neglected to take legal advice.

I heard Grandma relate her version so many times I could recite it along with her, usually to strangers we met on the bus or at the greengrocer. The last line was: 'We sold up and were swindled out of all our money and ended up living in two rooms in Greenford.' Nowhere in her telling did she blame my mother for falling for a property scam, nor did she admit her own misjudgement. As a child I was aware the details didn't add up, but it took a little longer to figure out why she took such satisfaction in recounting this particular story: Grandma saw herself as a victim of circumstance and needed the response it inevitably provoked.

Pity, however, doesn't sit well with pride, and Grandpa couldn't go back to Merthyr and admit they'd lost everything. Eventually, he found a live-in job as a caretaker at Hyde Park Street, round the corner from the flat I grew up in. From a position of authority on the buses, he was now polishing brass handrails, depositing post and newspapers through his employers' letterboxes and addressing them as 'Sir' and 'Your Grace'. Grandpa's civility was tinged with an air of defeat: the fight had gone out of him and he withdrew into a routine built around his afternoon nap. I don't think he ever forgave Grandma, or himself for not putting his foot down.

My mother left her bed-sit in Earl's Court and moved in with her parents and two younger siblings. She must have felt guilty having helped talk her father into losing his house and savings, but it didn't last long.

★ ★ ★

When I was a child, Grandma told me that my mother went travelling round the world on her own. 'Did she go *everywhere?*' I asked. 'Oh yes,' Grandma said. I imagined my bold, adventurous mother trekking through the desert, climbing the highest pyramid and braving the depths of a rainforest. I never saw her in towns or cities and she was always alone because Grandma had said so. These fantasy photos were as precious to me as the real ones: my mother was fearless and resourceful, crossing continents and bound-aries at a time when solo travel was mainly a masculine pursuit. Not only that, she financed her world tour on a secretary's salary.

The fantasy began to fade as soon as I realised, once again, that the details didn't quite fit. It all but disappeared when Howard told me how the trip came about. He saw an ad in the classified section of the *Evening Standard*: 'Female travel companion wanted, all expenses paid.' He thought it sounded fishy and showed it to my mother as a joke. He didn't think for a minute she'd take it seriously, but any number of reasons might have influenced her: escape from the strained atmosphere at home or a guilty conscience, or perhaps it was plain self-interest. Either way, she answered the ad and was gone within the week.

Likewise it's hard to guess how my grandparents felt, but they must have been disappointed as well as concerned: their previously comfortable, though quarrelsome, life was over, partly at my mother's instigation, and now she was off round the world with a stranger. 'Whatever Mum and Dad might have said wouldn't have made the blindest bit of difference,' Howard said. 'With Joan, it was jump first, think later.'

What happened next sounds as far-fetched as the most fanciful romantic fiction. It began with the ambiguous advertisement and ended in my mother's conversion to Catholicism. Her travelling companion's identity remained a mystery until two years ago when I came across his first name in one of my mother's letters to a later lover. She wrote that he was a wealthy Italian count named Jean-Baptiste and several years her senior. Their first stop was Fiesole, in the hills above Florence. So far it reads like the plot of a Mary Stewart novel — ingenuous girl in search of excitement falls for titled playboy in exotic location — but like the classic Stewart anti-hero, the count wasn't all he seemed.

They were married when she was twenty and began touring the Continent and Africa. My reveries of cocktail parties and ocean liners came to an abrupt halt as I read on: 'When we got to South Africa, he had a nervous breakdown, went berserk and was put into a strait-jacket in front of me. I haven't been able to sleep without pills since that moment.' It wasn't the first time my mother had stopped me in my tracks, but I hadn't expected the plot to shift so suddenly from romance to melodrama. She went back to Fiesole and never saw Jean-Baptiste again.

She described him as charismatic and loquacious, a gifted artist, and, most baffling of all, claimed the marriage was unconsummated. Her concise but frustratingly incomplete account left me with more questions than answers: Why did she go back to Italy instead of London? Did his lawyer pay her off? Was her charming, noble idler impotent as well as deranged? And, most importantly, was he still alive? The one answer she did give me was that her insomnia was triggered by emotional trauma.

I wrote to the Records Offices in Florence in search of a marriage certificate, and looked him up in *Libro d'Oro*, the Italian *Debrett's*, and various art libraries, with no results. Without a last name or location more specific than South Africa, finding Jean-Baptiste seemed an impossible task, until Howard told me that he'd lived in East London, a town on the coast about 600 miles south of Johannesburg. I went to Rhodes University website hoping an academic in the history department might have heard of Jean-Baptiste. I chose a name at random, Paul Maylam, and emailed him with the limited information I had so far. The next day I received the following: 'By a strange coincidence Jean-Baptiste Soffiantini was a client of my late father-in-law, George Randell, who was a solicitor in East London in the 1950s.' I've lost count how many times chance, intuition or blind luck have intervened in my research, but had I picked a different name my mother's first marriage might have remained a three-line anecdote in a letter.

Paul said his mother-in-law remembered

Jean-Baptiste well. Litigious, excitable and set on getting his own way, he caused her husband endless trouble with his constant legal demands. She said he lived in a castle of elaborate pillars and archways and once threatened to imprison George in the cellar.

Back on the Internet I found Jean-Baptiste was a local legend and his home an on-going curiosity. An estate agent's website described the turreted castle with its Juliet balcony as 'East London's most famous residential landmark, and surrounded by myth and mystery'. *Hi-Lite* magazine referred to the 'scandal attributed to its flamboyant and eccentric owner . . . according to newspaper reports, adorning the neglected castle walls were obscene murals painted by Jean-Baptiste of naked women.'

Amalie Niland, the journalist who'd written the *Hi-Lite* article, filled me in on his background: he was born in Florence and left Italy for South Africa in the 1930s after qualifying as a lawyer. A multi-millionaire, he made his fortune through property, stock market investments and perfume and hairdressing businesses, as well as producing films. He died in an asylum in 1978, aged eighty-nine.

In her letter my mother had written that he was older than her, but when I did the calculation I thought I must have got it wrong. I checked it twice: she was twenty when they married, he was sixty-two. I was as shocked by the forty-two-year age difference as I was by Jean-Baptiste's violent departure in a strait-jacket. The timing of his breakdown and their arrival at the castle were no accidents: the game was up. Not only had he abandoned a wife and two daughters in Italy, he had a common-law wife and four children in South Africa, as well as a succession of girlfriends. My mother mentioned none of this in her letter, but in less than a year she'd been duped again.

A week later Amalie emailed me a photograph of Jean-Baptiste, dated 1952 and taken at a local nightclub. Silver-haired, in a tuxedo and bow-tie with a glass of champagne in his hand, he looks like an Italian Omar Sharif. Sitting beside him was a glamorous young woman named Sheena Hewitt. I'd seen her name in the *Hi-Lite* article, which said she was a beauty queen and a model. With Amalie's help I tracked her down to Port Elizabeth.

Sheena was delightfully blunt and upfront when we spoke on the phone. Her description of Jean-Baptiste confirmed my mother's: 'He did indeed have great charm and finesse and he knew how to woo a woman, but he was only interested in very pretty, young girls.' She was nineteen when they met, the same age as my mother, but when he asked Sheena to marry him she had the sense to turn him down flat: 'He was too old and too mad.'

'He was a Jekyll and Hyde personality,' she said, 'like flicking a switch. He hid his pistols around the castle, and threatened to shoot me more than once.' During his psychotic episodes he would indeed lock people up in the cellar: 'He was like Bluebeard, and promised to incarcerate me if I ever betrayed him.' Sheena knew how to handle him, even with a gun at her head: 'The whole neighbourhood was afraid of Jean, but I stood up to him and knew how to talk him out of it.' In his defence, she added: 'He never actually shot anyone.'

A much tougher character than my mother, she was unfazed by his bouts of insanity: 'Like Van Gogh or Howard Hughes, he had the touch of the insane genius, but his greatest gift was for painting.' The supposedly obscene murals were portraits of Sheena with her bare backside showing.

He wasn't depressive or delusional but he had a deviant streak. 'He was more fantasist than charlatan,' she said. Erasing his past, 'Jean lived in the moment, and swore blind he had never been married.' Nor did he ever mention my mother to her, though they were almost contemporaries.

Sheena, among others, was certain his title was bogus. The Italians love to elevate anyone with flamboyance and front. If you look the part, you get the title to go with it, such as 'principe' or 'duca', 'dottore' or 'professore', regardless of lineage or qualifications: in Italy, plain old signor won't do. Jean-Baptiste not only looked the part, he had the fortune and the castle to go with it. When he and my mother were in Florence, he would have been addressed as 'Conte', and she would have had no reason to question it.

The more I found out about Jean-Baptiste the more it told me about my mother. I consulted a psychiatrist friend who told me his condition, with its symptoms of self-dramatisation, manipulativeness and possessiveness, exaggerated emotions and narcissism, sounded more like a histrionic personality disorder than a mental illness such as manic depression or schizophrenia. In layman's terms, my mother's acute reaction might have reflected her own susceptibility, so close to the surface there wasn't much to protect it. That she married such an older man brought with it all sorts of Freudian grace notes: Jean-Baptiste was the polar opposite of her almost silent father, not to mention nearly twenty years his senior.

There was no need for an annulment since the marriage was illegal. Abandoned in a strange Continent, my mother returned to Florence with the help of the British Consulate. My guess is she was too humiliated to go home and admit that all she had to show for her year with the count were insomnia and an empty wedding ring.

In just two years, my mother's life was remade by a series of disappointments and crises: leaving home for the big city, the vetoed marriage proposal from Mani, her part in the property swindle, and finally her disastrous misadventure with Jean-Baptiste. Locked up in the asylum, he had no idea he'd sentenced her to a lifelong addiction to barbiturates.

Back in Fiesole, my mother was distraught and unable to sleep. In the fallout from her marriage, she turned to the Church. Drawn to the dramatic and the colourful, she was more suited to the opulence and ritual of Catholicism than the stark observance of the unadorned Welsh chapel. In the midst of pain, suffering and confusion, the Catholic Church's rules and regulations must have seemed appealing.

The scent of incense and candle wax promised salvation, but one photograph of my mother suggests the opposite. In every photograph I have of her she's smiling, but this one conflicts with all the others. Standing in front of a cathedral, her face is framed in a black lace veil, her eyes hidden behind sunglasses. Her expression is tense and sombre and her gloved hands grip her wrists as if she's holding on for dear life. She seems to be facing some sort of *mea culpa*, and I can hardly bear to look at it.

Grandma didn't keep any of my mother's letters but she must have written to tell her the bad news. I wanted to know what she said, which details she shared and which she kept to herself, but most of all I wanted to know what she was feeling. In search of an answer I turned to my books, seventeen of which I inherited from my mother. Standing at the shelves in the hallway, I leafed through them, my eyes stinging with the dust of fifty-year-old pages foxed at the corners. I wasn't sure what I was looking for — a scribbled note in a margin or an unmailed postcard, anything that might indicate her state of mind. When I found it, my hand flew to my throat and I had to sit down. On the title page of *Song Offerings* by the Bengali writer Rabindranath Tagore, she'd written her name and the year, 1951. Towards the end of the book she'd marked one line in pencil: 'Mother, I shall weave a chain of pearls for thy neck with my tears of sorrow.'

6

The Publisher's Apprentice

In many ways my childhood was no different from my friends'. Normality came in the shape of Brownie badges or puzzling over why our Sindy dolls' hair didn't grow back when we cut it off. We played jacks and hopscotch on the pavement and our knees were permanently scraped from boisterous games of tag. In the late 1960s the only danger children faced on the streets was traffic, but I had one fear I couldn't share with my friends. Even though I knew it only happened to rich people, I was convinced I was about to be kidnapped.

Grandma still took me to school but I insisted on walking to my friends' houses on my own. Except I didn't walk, I sprinted. I'd leave our front doorstep as if it were a starting block and didn't stop until I crossed the finishing line. My anxiety wasn't entirely irrational. I knew from experience that children could be seized by law, but this was more visceral, as if somehow I'd been there before. Should the worst happen and I was bundled into the back of a car, I worked out a plan. I would talk my way out of it by telling the truth: my grandparents couldn't pay a ransom of more than a fiver. My potential captor would have no choice but to respond: 'Oh all right then, off you go.' It wasn't much of a plan but it was the best I could come up with at eight. After a few months the terror of abduction faded, but it left me with the feeling that fear is an invitation to show what you're made of, and even to show off your bravery.

Secure in the gated confines of Hampden Gurney, there was nothing to be scared of at primary school except for Johnny the playground thug. Lessons were no more demanding than basic sums, copying out poems by A.A. Milne and drawing pictures of London Bridge or the Post Office Tower. We had nothing to prove, no assessments or SATS, and league tables were for football teams not teachers. Our toughest assignment was the annual story-writing competition, which I won when I was nine. The prize was an Aztec chocolate bar. Nobody really liked Aztecs — they were full of raisins for one thing — but this one tasted like Mexican nectar. My story was about the adventures of a pony called Winny. I was well pleased with myself when I wrote the phrase 'metallic glint' to describe the sun catching on the buckle of her bridle. I loved playing with words and each new one felt like a shiny coin in an unlimited collection. The dictionary my father gave me on my seventh birthday was one of my most read books. I spent hours at a time flipping back and forth through its flimsy pages and it made me wonder if I might grow up to be a writer.

The ambition was soon squashed, ironically by his very last gift to me. A week before he died, my father put my name down for Christ's Hospital. Despite his dislike of Housey and its disciplinarian diktat, it had given him a sound education and he wanted the same for me. Perhaps he hoped the girls' school at Hertford would be staffed by teachers as inspirational and benevolent as D.S. Roberts. As it happened, our history teacher, Mrs Roxborough, was indeed cast in his mould. A few, however, were as lacklustre as Blam, and one or two as mean as Waddams and Macnutt.

I went to CH a year early, and at ten was one of the youngest in my class. I was unprepared for the leap from colouring with crayons and counting on an abacus to proper lessons with set books and tests. Even English was suddenly tricky as I lost my way within the grammatical maze. Struggling to keep up,

I failed most of my exams during the next four years. Like my mother, I was numerically challenged: I just about grasped Pythagoras' theorem but logarithms were pure torture. I only ever passed one maths exam, with 58 per cent — it's the one result I remember because it was so unexpected.

The standard of teaching at CH was no doubt above average, but at the time it didn't cater for the baffled child, who was left to founder. The refrain in my end-of-term reports was 'could try harder'. Had I known *how* to try harder I would have. I needed guidance, but when I asked my house-mistress for advice she said, 'Sit at the front of the class.' It didn't work. I wasn't getting any help at home either. It was beyond my grandparents' capability, and though I spent part of the school holidays with my aunt and uncle — Morticia and Gomez — the notion of encouragement wouldn't have occurred to them. Parenting at arm's length was more their style.

Miss Morrison, my English teacher, was old school and authoritarian. A no-nonsense Aberdonian, one of her favourite words was 'Sassenach', the Scots' slur for Saxon, but as she pointed out, we were sassenachs lower case. Her hair was pure white but she could have been any age between forty and sixty.

She weighed about twenty stone and wore navy blue suits made of a heavy-duty nylon material, her jacket stretched to bursting across her enormous bust and her skirt splitting at the seams. In the mid 1970s, she was known by the school wits as Boney M. and more accurately as Fatty M.

I was entranced by poetry from 'Jabberwocky' to the opium-induced 'Christabel'. When I put my hand up in class and asked how the latter might have differed without the influence of drugs, Fatty M. dismissed my question. 'You silly girl,' she snapped. 'It's of no relevance whatsoever.' Apparently I'd crossed some invisible line, but I never stopped asking awkward questions — I wanted to know why Byron was 'mad, bad and dangerous to know' and why Siegfried Sassoon had never married — but Fatty M. refused to expand on the salacious side of the poetic life, though she did tell me I had a delinquent mind.

Saturday morning prep was almost a pleasure because I'd save my English homework for this two-hour session. I say 'almost' because I knew when my exercise book came back Fatty M.'s red pen would always dishearten: she never gave me a grade higher than C. Formidable as she was, by the fourth form I finally summoned up the courage to ask her why. She looked at me with haughty Brodiean disdain and said, 'Your father may have been a writer but that doesn't mean you are.' Fatty M. was no D.S. Roberts. After her crushing rebuke I stopped trying and didn't bother to finish reading the set works for O-level: *Romeo and Juliet, Animal Farm* and . . . I can't even remember the third. I scraped a C for English Language but failed Eng. Lit. I was written off as an academic disappointment and believed it for years.

A decade later, at twenty-six, I still thought I was talentless and fit only for waitressing or a dead-end office job. I didn't dare hope that I might have inherited even a hint of my father's writing talent. By now I was living in New York. In the States, university education is accessible and the curriculum and time-table flexible, but it took a lot for me to enrol on a literature course. I nearly chickened out: what if Fatty M. was right?

Professor Laura Brenner was renowned at the State University for rarely awarding an A. One of my finest moments ever occurred after mid-term exams. The following week, when our essays were handed back, I beamed when I saw my grade at the top of the first page: Professor Brenner had given me an A. After that, academia was plain sailing. I only stayed at university for two years: I didn't need to graduate since I'd already found what I was looking for. Either I was a late developer or Fatty M. had borne some sort of grudge. Three years ago I went to her memorial service knowing that my own grudge had disappeared the second I'd proved her wrong.

My time at CH wasn't all botched exams and indifferent support. I soon recognised that there were benefits to my unusual family situation; the disadvantages were harder to admit so I put them to one side. My friends initially reacted to my background with curiosity, then a touch of envy: with no parents to answer to, I was free to misbehave far more than they were. By fourteen, misbehaviour was what I did best.

The school was enclosed within a high wall crowned with barbed wire and broken glass. Escape involved stealth and cunning, especially after lights-out. On more than one occasion, Fiona B. and I 'borrowed' the housemistress's key to the back gate. Security was less of a concern in the 1970s, and she kept her keys in the pocket of her coat which hung beside the door to her sitting room. Tiptoeing on platform shoes down the darkened stairs from upper dorm, Fiona and I swiped the keys, clambered through a window in the day room and crept out for a nocturnal adventure at the visiting funfair. We flirted with the bad boys showing off on the bumper cars and squealed when the carny on the waltzer shouted, 'Scream if you want to go faster.' Giddy with adrenaline and queasy after scoffing hot dogs and candy floss, when we got back to House well after midnight, Lyn R.W. said, 'I wouldn't dream of doing half the things you do; my dad would kill me.'

Aside from the thrill we derived from evading punishment, most of my wayward friends shared a secondary rationale for disobedience: an absent father on his third marriage, a mother more concerned with her martini intake than her daughter's welfare and one or two pernicious and self-seeking divorces. My parents were dead, theirs didn't care. It's hard to say which was worse.

My transgressions were minor, aside from one or two in my last year. I'd acquired a handful of home-grown dope along with instructions on how to dry it. During a free afternoon when I was supposed to be revising for O-levels, I wrapped the raw leaves in tin foil and cooked them under the grill in the house kitchen, which was out of bounds except for breaktime. One of the cleaners came in and asked what I was doing.

'Homework,' I said. 'It's a chemistry experiment.' The smell of toasting weed should have given me away but she seemed satisfied with my answer and went off to polish the parquet. Late that night, I rolled a joint and lit it as I leaned out of the bathroom window. It smelled fusty and tasted like penicillin mould on week-old bread, and I flushed the rest of my stash down the loo. My abortive experiment put me off dope for years.

Whether bunking off maths, fermenting undrinkable cider in the basement of the science block or sneaking my first boyfriend into the fifth-form study at midnight, I was skilfully naughty and was rarely caught. It was as if the gods were compensating for my inauspicious start in life by allowing me more than my fair share of mischief.

★   ★   ★

My father was also naughty at school, but precocious with it. At fifteen he sent his first play to the controller of the BBC's Radio Drama department. He received a polite but encouraging rejection. After he left Housey, he submitted an original radio play, *Professional Conduct*, co-written with Tony Tighe. It was broadcast on 29 August 1942. From then on he was a regular contributor, as both writer and presenter, to various radio departments.

The BBC's Written Archives Centre in Reading holds seven hefty files on my father, from 1938 to 1957. More than any other source, the correspondence, contracts and memos provided a timeline of his professional life from Housey to his final address, a bed-sit in Shepherd's Bush. The last file, dated 1958-67, is thin and its contents all rejections.

Towards the end of 1939, his apprenticeship at the advertising agency was interrupted when he was seconded by the Admiralty to Bristol as a civilian employee undertaking routine clerical duties. He stayed with Great Aunt Frances nearby in Bath. By now she was in her late seventies and dottier than ever. Uncle John said she was a batty old spinster and a nosy so-and-so, but my father was intrigued by eccentric characters, especially one who might spill a few of the Hyde-Clarke beans. If she let slip details of his mother's paternity or his grandmother's gallivanting, he didn't tell anyone else in the family, which was another reason why he was so easy to confide in; he loved gossip but didn't feel the need to pass it on.

Even the neighbours steered clear of Frances but I'd like to think my father's companionship over Sunday afternoon tea or a sherry before dinner brought her a little comfort. Within the year, however, he was back in London and Frances was alone again in her big, empty house. Not long after he left, she began to deteriorate. Her decline culminated in her drafting a new will leaving her entire estate to her solicitor. A week later, she gassed herself. It's impossible to say how many, or perhaps how few, mourners attended her funeral, but I'm sure my father was among them.

He returned to his apprenticeship at the advertising agency in September 1940, at the moment the Battle of Britain commenced. By November, a quarter of the capital's population had fled for the countryside. During the Blitz the city was bombed almost every night for nine months. Sleep was something Londoners could only daydream about. The lack of it drove many half mad, together with the terror that came with the wail of the air-raid siren, the drone of incoming bombers and the ack-ack of anti-aircraft guns. They woke up, if they'd managed to sleep at all, to the sounds and smells of a city damaged but defiantly unbroken. Glass crunched underfoot and water gushed from burst mains, scorched brick dust and cordite burned the back of the throat, sewers and gas pipes

130

leaked, but worst of all were the swarms of flies signposting bodies buried beneath smouldering rubble. Only the rats and the looters thrived.

At the start of the Blitz the government had forbidden the use of Tube stations as shelters, but it couldn't stop anyone with a platform ticket for a halfpenny riding the escalator down to safety. After a few months, only 4 per cent of Londoners bothered with the Underground. Fed up with the discomfort and unsanitary conditions, the rest took their chances at home, in an Anderson shelter in the garden or under the dining room table. During particularly heavy bombing raids my father and his parents took refuge in the basement at Emperor's Gate.

Topsy was out of work for much of the war. He painted the occasional miniature but no one had the money for a full-scale portrait. When they were young, both John and my father used to sit beside him for hours as he stooped over a tiny piece of ivory with his magnifying glass and a brush made of a single hair. Essentially they were watching paint dry, but in Topsy's company it was a fascinating process.

Inventive but inexperienced, his money-making schemes were rarely successful. Among his most enterprising was the cultivation of a mushroom farm in the cellar. It was a two-fold profit plan: after harvesting, the spent compost (known as gardeners' gold) was far more lucrative, the mushrooms being a by-product. Topsy muddled through the delicate and labour intensive process, planting spawn in boxes of peat and horse manure shovelled up on the street. The temperature should be around 70°F and the environment sterile, but like most cellars theirs was full of old paint pots and household debris. Combined with the heat of a particularly humid summer, the contaminated air and the mushrooms caused a spontaneous combustion. At around the time Barnes Wallis was working on his plans for the bouncing bomb, Topsy's secret weapon was the exploding fungus. Smoke damage aside, no harm was done but the over-worked Fire Service had a quiet word and put an end to Topsy's agricultural experiments.

Despite my father's pacifism and his mother's objections, he tried to enlist. His brother John was now serving as a medical officer with the British First Army in North Africa. Gwendolyn had no qualms waving him off with his kitbag but she still treated my father like a fragile five-year-old; she told him he was already wounded, a comment that can't have done much for his self-esteem.

When he was inevitably classified unfit for military service because of his eyesight, the rejection left him feeling he had a lot to prove, but he would have to wait another five years.

In mid 1941, aged eighteen, he began working as a trainee in the production department at Faber and Faber in Russell Square. It was a significant move to one of the country's most venerable publishing houses and, as he'd predicted when he left Housey, more of a tertiary education than a job.

During the war the larger publishers managed a steady but greatly reduced output. Smaller houses, along with numerous literary journals, folded when paper was rationed from 1940. It was sometimes acquired by surreptitious methods, but Faber had a legitimate advantage: one of its former directors worked for American Intelligence and used this connection to obtain sufficient paper. Print runs were short but demand outstripped supply; desperate for imaginative outlets, the public read voraciously and whatever was published sold out. Literature became a national diversion: libraries had never been busier, as were subscription services such as the one run by Boots the chemist; voluntary organisations collected second-hand books for the troops — in all, donations amounted to 56 million volumes. With extraordinary foresight, Allen Lane at Penguin published the first paperbacks in 1935; the price remained at sixpence until 1942 when it shot up to ninepence. The surviving journals, including *Horizon*, *New Writing* and the *TLS*, were a just-about affordable luxury and passed around samizdat-style until they fell apart.

Even today, the production department is sometimes taken for granted, as if it's subservient to editorial, yet it's the bedrock of any publishing house. My father learned his trade from the foundations up, from scheduling and distribution to estimates and jacket design. He was especially fascinated by the intuitive elements of typography; he believed each typeface had its own personality and voice and spoke to the reader in the tone of the text. When I studied the styles of the period side by side, I saw what he meant: Plantin strikes me as chubby and chipper, Perpetua polite but shrewd and Scotch gluttonous and a touch overbearing. I've never really taken to the slender but grudging Times New Roman; one of the most common yet least admired, it resentfully conceded the greatest legibility within the smallest space. The face of the printed page also changed as margins shrank to conserve paper; in the interests of economy, particularly verbose authors were tactfully asked to 'do their bit' and reduce the length of their manuscripts. In spite of these constraints, through artful layout and typesetting, the text within a Faber title never looked cramped or hard on the eye.

My father worked alongside a master typographer, the art director Berthold Wolpe, who also joined the company in 1941. He was a gentle and patient teacher, and in the congenial atmosphere of the production department, everyone, from my father up to Mr Wolpe, contributed to a book's overall design. There was no budget and luckily no need for advertising, and as the sole promotional tool the cover had to say a lot more within straitened means. While other publishers were keen to signal their commitment to wartime measures, Faber maintained standards and Wolpe's hand-drawn lettering was instantly recognisable, elegant and unfussy but never austere. Seeing a volume through from raw copy to book-seller's shelf, my father was acutely aware that production was primarily concerned with tailoring the author and his words in a jacket that best suits them both.

Pre-eminent among Faber's directors was

T.S. Eliot. Dignified and seemingly unapproachable, he was revered as a cultural authority, but my father didn't do hero-worship or sycophancy. When they occasionally exchanged a few words as they passed in the corridor it was always at my father's instigation. Lean, lanky and bespoke-suited with a dangling pocket watch, Eliot was only fifty-three, but poets of his era seemed to age prematurely. In contrast to his imperious reputation, he was a practical joker and his sense of humour as keen as Colman's mustard. For the erudite and urbane, high jinks provided a diversion from the world of serious publishing. I was delighted to discover that he shared with my father an appreciation for the surreal silliness of the Marx Brothers films.

Tony Tighe told me he went to see my father at Faber's offices one evening after everyone had gone home. Like schoolboys breaking into the tuck shop, they picked the lock of Eliot's attic office and nosed among his papers while listening to his recording of *The Waste Land*. 'Little Gidding' was published in 1942; unknown to the poet, my father might well have been one of the first to read it.

During the Blitz, incendiary bombs were as dangerous as high explosives and on the rooftops of London fire-watching was crucial duty. Eliot's fire-watching night was Tuesday. It's not easy to picture his playful side but I can imagine him and my father on the summit of the Faber building: two intellectual beanpoles acting out the mirror routine from the Marx Brother's *Duck Soup*, with Eliot as Groucho and my father as Harpo imitating his every move.

Faber dominated poetry and published it profitably and without subsidy; as one of today's few independent publishers it still does. Its list included Robert Graves, Louis MacNeice and W.H. Auden. Under the influence of such heavyweights, my father's one surviving notebook, dated 1942, contains four of his poems, their theme a young man's yearning for perfect love. They're as callow and clumsy as the verse I wrote at around the same age. Neither of us has an ear for it, though I find my father's rather endearing:

In the midnight hours I find no sleep
And all my heart and mind on you do
    rest.
Thinking of fruit I will never reap
Like treasure in an ever closed chest.
And soon the magics of that dream dis-
    solve
Leaving me yet with sadness still to
    solve.

137

The untitled poem was inspired by one of his first serious girlfriends: again, a third party complicated, or perhaps simplified, the relationship. His school friend John Mayes remembers my father introducing him to an older woman he worked with at Faber whose fiancé was serving overseas. John was impressed and a little concerned that, at nineteen, my father's love life was already so convoluted.

One of his first prose pieces appeared in the winter 1944 edition of the literary journal *The Wind and the Rain*. Its title is 'A Romantic Story' and it opens: ' . . . his tall, dishevelled figure, with deep set eyes and death-white skin, his long black cloak falling off one shoulder and gathering dust as he walked. He did not care if they stared at him as he went by and whispered to each other, or that mothers warned their daughters against him. He was perversely delighted with his reputation.' Aside from the dishevelled outfit and death-white skin there's more than a note of autobiography here. The journal was edited by the late Neville Braybrooke who told me: 'Your father was a bit of a rake and I can rarely remember him without a girlfriend or two. Somehow he always managed to talk himself out of trouble.' His reputation together with his appearance, is often the first thing his friends recall.

Clothes rationing was introduced in 1941 but I doubt my father ever wore what was dubbed the Austerity Suit — single-breasted jacket with shallow pockets and trousers without turn-ups. 'Michael was a sharp dresser and never looked scruffy,' John Mayes said. 'He invariably wore a tweed sports coat, V-neck pullover and woollen tie in a thick knot, flannels, brown brogues and a gabardine raincoat. It was the publishing uniform in those days, with Stephen Spender as its exemplar.' It's said men tend to stick with the style of their early twenties, especially if it advertises a profession they're proud of. My father obviously wasn't slave to evolving fashion trends; more than twenty-five years later, I remember him wearing a heavy raincoat and big brown shoes.

'He sometimes wore a black eye patch,' John went on, 'which added a piratical edge to the image. For some reason, women found it particularly appealing.' Like a walking stick it served a requisite purpose in announcing vulnerability — in blustery weather a piece of grit in his good eye would leave him temporarily blind, the patch alerting a passer-by to stop and help him. It also provoked curiosity. When a prospective girlfriend asked about the patch, he would pause and say, 'It's a long story … ' It excused his civilian status and allowed her a fleeting fantasy of cloak and dagger and derring-do.

Most of my father's contemporaries had joined up, leaving him in the company of a somewhat older generation. He had a gift for what we now call networking and began to form friendships with the next wave of poets, including Dylan Thomas, John Lehmann and the Tamil eccentric Tambimuttu who, along with many others, helped advance my father's early career.

Stealing him away from Faber after two productive years, Tambimuttu offered him an editorial post at his magazine *Poetry (London)*, published by Nicholson and Watson. It was one of the leading periodicals of its time and younger poets, including Kathleen Raine, Lawrence Durrell and (my father's Housey nemesis) Keith Douglas, appeared alongside de la Mare, Eliot and Auden. Tambi was greatly admired for his foresight and risk-taking in spotting new talent, if not for his professionalism. At the magazine's Manchester Square offices his desk was a toppling mass of drafts, galleys and unanswered correspondence. My father's by contrast was orderly and his copy-editing and proof-reading meticulous. Tambi's working methods were famously chaotic; he frequently mislaid manuscripts in taxis and bars and showed no regard for schedules or deadlines. Fortunately, he had the sense to surround himself with a loyal and tolerant staff who all mucked in with typing and packing up boxes for distribution as well as arranging contracts and royalties. My father found Tambi's slack attitude infuriating but his exuberance and genius as a literary catalyst more than made up for it.

Tambi preferred to conduct business at the pub and was out of the door well before opening time, his siren call the imminent jangling of a landlord's keys. My father usually stayed late, making up for missed deadlines. At night the city was like a stage set just after the house lights go down. With his hands outstretched to avoid colliding with fellow pedestrians, he followed Tambi's well-worn route from Manchester Square to Fitzrovia through hushed and pitch-black streets free of traffic, the only illumination from the moon or the illicit flash of a match. On the other side of the pub black-out curtain, my father and Tambi made quite a pair: one flaxen and neatly combed, the other with long, unwashed black hair, looking like a shabbily dressed eastern prince in a voluminous overcoat, which he rarely discarded.

With so few single young men in London out of uniform, they were never short of female company. Tambi's affairs were as brief and torrid as my father's, but his approach was less discreet and certainly less mannerly. With disarming dark eyes and a persuasive line in seduction, few women were put off by this presumptuous, grubby-looking scruff. Unaccustomed to rejection, Tambi was ungracious in defeat, like a foul-mouthed child denied a promised toy. Spotlight and scandal were two of his favourite words, and in nicely spoken literary circles his effing and blinding turned heads and occasionally averted noses. The more he drank the more voluble and querulous he became, but his tantrums were short-lived and always entertaining.

For Tambi and his entourage, the Wheatsheaf in Rathbone Place was one of several unofficial headquarters, where Dylan Thomas would regularly try to sell his coat to my father for the price of a drink. In the 1940s Fitzrovia stretched from Fitzroy Street south to Old Compton Street, the territory marked by Finch's the One Tun and the York Minster. It's shrunk over the years, but the Wheatsheaf is still there; wood-panelled, fake-beamed with leaded glass windows and gloomy lighting, it remains a pint-and-a-smoke kind of pub. On the wall by the corner of the bar hang framed newspaper cuttings celebrating the likes of George Orwell, Julian Maclaren-Ross and Dylan Thomas. There is no mention of Tambi, one of its most influential and benevolent former residents. If his memory lingers at all, it's as a champion of up-and-coming talent at the expense of his own.

Drinking and writing went hand in hand, but alcohol was never my father's crutch. Unlike many of his friends, he was a lightweight and could make a pint last the whole evening. Uncle John was home on leave for my father's twenty-first birthday party in 1944: 'I brought a few bottles of black-market Algerian plonk. Michael got terribly drunk and had to be put to bed. He was sick as a dog the next day and never let me forget it.' Driven and diligent as he was, it was probably his last hangover.

For Tambi money was more of a nuisance than a necessity and it spent as little time as possible in his pocket. Entertaining at home was more pot-luck than dinner party. My father's niece Sheila was a teenager at the time and remembers the informal gatherings at Tambi's: 'He lived in a tall house near Camden where he and Michael sometimes hosted parties. I say hosted, but by 8 p.m. Tambi was like an untamed creature dancing around and singing calypso songs at the top of his voice.' Sheila used to make the sandwiches and serve the drinks but, with avuncular concern, my father told her to avoid the top floor because that's where the drugs were. Drugs weren't widespread in the 1940s and were generally beyond the bohemian budget. Tambi, however, would happily squander his last few quid on marijuana and cocaine. Sheila said my father probably tried both but, unlike Tambi, he preferred to stay in control.

He didn't do drugs for the same reason he didn't drink much: he was following his vocation and everything else in his life, including girlfriends, took second place. His friend Anne Valery wryly noted a mindset typical of the era: 'Michael's generation of literary young men were ruthlessly ambitious and took themselves very seriously — their work was spelled with a capital W.'

When my father's contemporaries returned to civilian life in 1945, he had a six-year head start. He was contributing the occasional book review to the *Sunday Times* and the *TLS* and had at least eleven radio broadcasts to his credit, mostly adaptations of novels and plays including James Joyce's *The Dead* and Max Beerbohm's *Poor Romeo*. At twenty-three, my father already knew how to negotiate the crossroads and roundabouts of literary London and his writing career began in earnest the following year.

The publisher and poet John Lehmann was among the most distinguished of my father's contacts. A partner with Leonard and the late Virginia Woolf at the Hogarth Press and the brother of novelist Rosamond Lehmann, he was also editor of *Penguin New Writing* and later the *London Magazine*. Alongside his freelancing, my father worked part-time for Lehmann who assumed the role of semi-patron, introducing him to the great and the good and recommending memberships to the correct clubs, including the Reform and the Travellers and the less reputable Woolly Lamb and Gargoyle. Lehmann was one of his first homosexual friends; it didn't hurt that my father was an attractive and sphinx-like young man who liked to court curiosity. Ulterior motive or not, over the years Lehmann continued to keep a paternal watch over his protégé.

Like a worse-for-wear fairy godmother, Dylan Thomas tripped, or stumbled, in and out of my father's early career. They'd first met at Faber, and as a founding editor of *Poetry (London)*, it was Thomas who introduced him to Tambi. During the war Thomas was a prolific scriptwriter for the BBC, and he and my father often ran into each other at the Gluepot pub in Mortimer Street, the mandatory annexe to Broadcasting House. The beer-soaked banter and pledging of overcoats soon grew wearisome; heavy drinking was all very well, but witnessing a slow self-destruction was a sight my father found unbearable and he would cross the road or duck into a doorway to avoid him. Thomas, however, had one last gift to bestow.

Along with covering his professional and social bases, my father had a knack for finding himself in the right place at the right time. One afternoon in 1946, on the steps of the Reform Club in Pall Mall, he ran into Thomas and his BBC colleague Douglas Cleverdon, who would later produce *Under Milk Wood*. 'Do you know anything about Henry James?' Cleverdon asked my father; he was working on a radio programme about James and urgently needed a writer-presenter. 'Everything,' my father replied. 'He's one of my favourite authors.' He got the job there and then. On his way home, he stopped at the London Library and withdrew three of James's best-known works and F.O. Matthiesen's critical study. He stayed up all night and read through the lot. Years later, he owned up to Douglas Cleverdon that when they first met he knew almost nothing about

James and had read only one of his novels at school. With his photographic memory, he became an overnight, if patchy, authority. My father's opportunism marked the beginning of a lifelong and fruitful fascination with the Master, though his influence wasn't entirely beneficial.

7

'Falling Slowly'

Like my parents, it seems I wasn't destined for a quiet, comfortable life. Disruption was the norm and since I had nothing to compare it with, the setbacks and impediments rarely took me by surprise. The most unforeseen, and still unresolved, obstacle occurred during the summer term of 1975 when I was fourteen. My friends and I were playing leap frog on the sports field when one of them shrieked, 'Yuk, look at Anna's back!' We ran across the square to House and up two flights to upper dorm. Standing with my back to the full-length mirror, I turned my head and saw that the right side of my ribcage was so bowed it looked deformed. I had no idea what might have caused it. I hadn't tripped and landed awkwardly in hockey practice or fallen off the beam in gym. More puzzled than alarmed, the next morning I went to see the school doctor, thinking he would push my ribs back into place and that would be the end of it. After examining me he said he would make an appointment for me with a

My father, aged five, taken shortly before the eye accident in 1928.

My mother and her brother Howard, Merthyr Tydfil, 1933.

Topsy's portrait of my
father, 1939.

My father and Iliana
von Fraunberg at the
opera house in Florence,
1950.

My father and Carib friend,
Guyana, 1955.

My father, 1957.

My mother in the fallout of her first marriage, Italy, 1951.

Sheena Hewitt and Jean-Baptiste Soffiantini (my mother's first husband), 1952.

My mother, late 1950s.

My mother in her (second) wedding dress, 1958.

My parents on their wedding day, 1958.

My mother and me, Majorca, 1961.

Kay Dick, the portentous portrait my mother first saw in Raleigh Trevelyan's office.

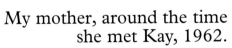

My mother, around the time she met Kay, 1962.

Grandma, Grandpa and me, 1963.

Me, Trafalgar Square, 1964.

My father, mid 1960s.

Grandma and me, 1961.

School photo, 1966.

My cousin David, 1966.

Grandpa on the beach at
Llansteffan, *c*.1960s.

The summer before my banishment from the first Castle Greyskull, 1978.

New York, 1988 – the year I began writing my parents' story as a novel.

specialist and that I might need an operation. I left the infirmary thoroughly alarmed.

A couple of months later I went to the Orthopaedic Hospital near Great Portland Street, accompanied by the school nurse. On the train to London I asked her if they'd make me have surgery there and then. 'I shouldn't think so, dear,' she said. It wasn't the reassuring response I was hoping for. Sitting in the out-patients waiting room I was surrounded by children in callipers and neck braces. A few were propped up in wheel-chairs. Aside from a wonky back, I was fit and healthy and I felt like a fraud. The boy opposite me had a cage-like contraption screwed into his skull and collarbone. I felt sorry for him but I didn't want him to see it; he'd probably had enough pitying glances by now to last a lifetime. I looked down at my shoes and saw that one of his was a black surgical boot with a four-inch sole. I closed my eyes and tried not to picture myself leaving the hospital imprisoned in some gruesome instrument of torture.

In the consulting room I was weighed and measured and the doctor asked me a lot of medical questions. I blew into a tube to test my lung capacity, touched my toes and stretched to left and right. Then he sent me to radiology. When he placed my X-ray on the

149

light box I stared at it and frowned: I couldn't figure out what it was, but it looked like a snake in the shape of a perfect S. 'What is it?' I asked. 'It's your spine,' he said. The spectral image of my sinuous vertebrae made me feel faint and I had to sit down.

He told me I had idiopathic adolescent scoliosis. Curvature of the spine is a common condition — around 10 per cent of the population have it in varying extents — but mine was acute, more than 45 degrees. The doctor outlined the only option, an operation during which he'd remove slivers of bone from my pelvis and insert them between my vertebrae to shore up the curve, with no guarantee that it wouldn't progress. I'd be flat on my back in a plaster cast from my chest to my hips for ten months. 'And we'll have to repeat the surgery every five years,' he added. 'Shall I put you on the waiting list?' Aside from losing nearly a year of school, it wasn't the fear of the surgeon's scalpel or the consequent pain that made up my mind — I didn't even think of the scars — it was the thought of Grandma's reaction that gave me my answer. In less than a split second I said, 'No thank you.'

Owing to a bureaucratic mishap, it was several months before my grandparents were informed. Hospital was Grandma's acme of drama and disaster, and a prospective spinal operation would provide enough sympathetic attention to gratify her for at least ten months. Knowing she would try to persuade me to put my name on the hospital waiting list, I kept the orthopaedic development to myself. When I eventually underwent surgery twenty years later the procedure had advanced immeasurably, but Grandma's ghost hovered in the operating theatre. I woke up in Intensive Care an inch and a half taller but with a virulent infection. Three operations later I was left with a sixteen-inch scar and far more back pain than when I started.

Unlike my mother and her younger siblings, I had no desire to play the sickly child. For one thing, illness got in the way of tennis and squash and roller-skating. I saw nothing remarkable or engaging in a hacking cough or a runny nose, but for Grandma, caring for the delicate and ailing was the ultimate expression of love. Selfless as it seemed, I was forewarned by the whiff of a martyr burning and denied her the pleasures of clucking and fussing around the sickbed. I was a disappointment to her in that respect, but still her favourite.

Grandma was as warm as toast when she chose to be, but frosty in her unpredictable prejudices. She had little time for Howard's

151

two children and even less for my cousin David. She told him he was too slow to catch a cold, even though he learned to read before I did and was a natural with a paint brush. My crayon efforts looked like infantile scrawls next to his intelligently composed artwork, yet she couldn't bring herself to praise him. With his big brown eyes he looked more like Grandma than the rest of the cousins, but even on birthdays she showed her disapproval: I was given half-a-crown, David two shillings.

What she most deplored was his clumsiness, her dictum 'Don't touch that, you'll break it,' recited like a catchphrase. Not surprisingly, David was also accident-prone and his visits to Hyde Park Gardens frequently ended in a trip to Casualty for stitches or a tetanus shot. In place of a kiss and a cuddle he got a telling-off and a slap. It was far worse at home with Morticia and Gomez. Their house was spotless and the decor fashionably bland, with everything in its place and an ambient temperature several degrees below convivial. It reminded me of a Habitat showroom. Mealtimes were not considered social events and were near enough silent to make a Trappist monk flush with approval.

The only emotion Gomez conveyed with

any conviction was anger, a rage so close to the surface it barely needed a trigger. He also had a few things in common with the Housey tyrants, including cowardice; I wish I'd had the nerve to say, 'Pick on someone your own size.' It seemed his particular breed of bully needed no more than one target at a time and I was relieved I wasn't on the receiving end. My turn came shortly after David made his escape at seventeen. After leaving Christ's Hospital for the sixth form at Camden School for Girls, it was decided that since my grandparents were now seventy I should live with Morticia and Gomez at the first Castle Greyskull, in Maida Vale. It wasn't long before I felt like an inconvenient guest.

For some people Christmas is like Sundays, but with presents. For me it's the least welcome day of the year. A few weeks before my first Christmas at Castle Greyskull, Gomez announced that he and Morticia were spending the holidays in Marbella. As if it were a business meeting he was unable to accommodate he told me I should make alternative arrangements. I'd spent enough time with them over the years to know that the tree would be artificial (avoiding the mess of fallen pine needles), the turkey and sprouts accompanied by a small glass of wine and — a vestige of Welsh chapel temperance

— Black Magic chocolates meted out individually, with the silent mantra 'just the one'. It wasn't that I was anticipating joyful Fezziwig festivities but my Yuletide exclusion left me feeling like the little match girl. It remains a snow-blind, Dickens-cum-Andersen memory.

I did, however, appropriate a special gift that year. Grandma told me that the pearl ring I'd played with as a child was my mother's engagement ring, which I'd assumed was from my father. Now that I know he was penniless when they married it was more likely to be Jean-Baptiste's. It didn't fit me until I was sixteen, when I wore it on the fourth finger of my right hand. It was old-fashioned and more suited to a Knightsbridge deb, but I didn't care how silly it looked with my threadbare Levi's torn at the knees and a leopard-skin boob tube; in 1977 there was a certain charm in contrasting the sublime with the ridiculous. After a year or so the iridescent surface rubbed away leaving a dull white sphere in a gold-plated setting. My mother wore the ring for only a few months and wouldn't have known that the pearl was as fake as her first marriage.

★　★　★

In 1951, armed with her new-found faith, my mother left Florence and moved back in with the family at Hyde Park Gardens. Around this time she worked as a secretary to the philosopher Karl Popper at the London School of Economics. Popper's atheism and my mother's fervent conversion to Catholicism should have made for heated debate, but now that I know she was softly spoken and compliant I can't hear her arguing her side.

Such feminine self-effacement is illustrated in the films of the era, and none more so than Doris Day's. As a role model for the single girl, she was sugary-sweet and sometimes feisty, but only up to a point. Before the credits rolled, she was shown the error of her ways and persuaded to surrender her professional ambitions for love. During the war women found they were more than capable of fulfilling traditionally masculine jobs, but by the mid 1950s it was as if the brief period of emancipation had never happened. The genie was coaxed back into her bottle, or kitchen, by an industry run by men. The message was loud and clear: it would remain a man's world if the chaps had anything to do with it. Sugared, biddable Doris in propaganda films such as *Pillow Talk* and *That Touch of Mink* played by the rules.

As much as I hate to say it, it seems my mother was as easily influenced by cinema as she was by literature. The years between her two marriages — 1951-8 — remain an enigma, as if she were a cipher defined by the men in her life. Had she lived to see the 1970s, I doubt she would have fought for a place at the forefront of the feminist cause.

She wrote the occasional book review for *The Times*, submitted under the pseudonym Leigh Adams. Always on the move, she worked as a sub-editor for the *Radio Times*, as a reader for a publishing house and in the editorial department of the Bureau of Hygiene and Tropical Medicine, one of the few jobs she stuck at. Among the journals she worked on was the *Bulletin of Hygiene* — Grandma would have loved that.

My mother created an androgynous and class-free identity, but she covered her tracks too well; *The Times* reviews were unsigned until 1966 and Leigh Adams has proved impossible to trace without knowing which books she reviewed. As Joan Howells she was just as ephemeral. Grandma may have exaggerated when she told me my mother studied philosophy at the LSE. Its archives hold no record of her enrolment, and it's more likely she attended a few of Popper's lectures. There was also no sign of her in the personnel archives of the *Radio Times* or the Bureau of Hygiene and Tropical Medicine. It may simply be down to erratic record-keeping, but it's as if she barely existed.

Reflecting cinema's attitude, magazines such as *Good Housekeeping* and the *Lady* catered for the woman who knew her place was in the home. Institutions such as the BBC weren't alone in their strict 'marriage bar' policy for female employees: engagement meant imminent redundancy. By the late 1950s the cinched waist of a dirndl skirt was worn in anticipation of a maternity frock. The editors of those corseted magazines would have consigned my mother, at twenty-seven, to the proverbial shelf.

Faced with these contradictions, I wanted her to be the maverick who broke with convention rather than the chameleon who changed her colours, and her name, to blend in. The woman she'd invented was so opaque I think she'd lost sight of the real Joan.

I'd lost sight of her too. So far my main source of information was family, but I needed a more objective view. As has happened so frequently during the writing of this book, it came to me by chance. Two years ago, I wrote an article for the *Mail on Sunday* magazine about the ghost relation ship between parents who die too young and the children they leave behind. It ran with several photographs of my parents, and I asked the editor to add my email address at the end of the piece in the hope that someone who had known my mother might see it. Two months later I received the response I'd been waiting for: 'I was flicking through an old copy of *You* magazine when I saw a face that reminded me of a friend I had many years ago. On turning another page, I realised that it wasn't just a passing resemblance . . . the baby I knew at just a few weeks had written the article.'

Dot Barclay worked with my mother at the Bureau and kept in touch until she left England for a working holiday a few months before my mother died in 1962. We met for lunch on the day London reached a record summer temperature. Even the climate contributed a small detail: 'Joan would have hated this weather. She didn't like bright sunshine and wore dark glasses even when it was cloudy.' It was Dot who told me that private lives remained private, and she knew little about my mother's first husband: 'All Joan said was that he was a bigamist and had lots of girlfriends. She had terrible taste in men, but I think it was down to her sympathetic streak — she saw a man in need and wanted to help make him better. And of course your father was the ultimate challenge in that respect.

'Joan would walk into the office with a big smile and a cheery hello,' Dot said. 'I keep coming back to it but she was always smiling. At the time I didn't realise it masked such unhappiness.' Dot gave me five postcards she'd received from my mother, written during her marriage to my father. They're as brief and uninformative as emails: 'Just visited the Picasso exhibition — marvellous — to my surprise!' 'Longing to see you and give you all my news and hear yours!' Her breezy tone and frequent exclamation marks concealed the unhappiness as effectively as her smile.

I asked Dot to describe my mother's voice: 'She had no trace of a Welsh accent, but on the rare occasions when she talked about anything personal her voice would become softer and softer and you had to lean towards her to hear what she was saying.' During the last few months of their friendship my mother's life was in chaos and her dependency on prescription drugs escalating. The frailty in her voice may have been a result of both.

When I asked if my mother talked about her ambitions as a writer, Dot couldn't remember her ever mentioning them. One recollection, however, set me off on a particularly charged quest: 'Joan went to see David Attenborough regarding a broadcast she was about to give. I think it might have been for *Woman's Hour*.' I wrote to David Attenborough, Jenni Murray at *Woman's Hour*, various BBC departments and every radio archive I could find, with no luck so far. I had the feeling the sound of my mother's voice might be lost to me for ever.

Along with everyone else I've spoken to, Dot had as many questions as I did, and I'm surprised to find I have most of the answers. It also occurred to me that despite the missing pieces I probably know more about my parents than anyone. I had no trouble finding my father through his friends and published work, but my mother left so little of either that I've had to step into her size five stilettos. They fit, but they're uncomfortable and I can't walk more than a few steps in them. Constricted by society's expectations, she had far fewer choices than I do; unfairly and unreasonably, I demanded too much of her. Culture and convention determined my mother's path, while barbiturates ensured instability and unrest. The mirror is now cracked; it still reflects my mother's face but I identify with her in one respect only. The unwelcome trait we share was triggered by traumatic events: my mother's at twenty, by the Crazy Count, mine at thirty-three, by spinal surgery.

Insomnia plays tricks on the mind. Minor concerns loom out of proportion and thoughts revolve and collide in a warped kaleidoscope. Any insomniac with an important decision to make in the morning knows better than to follow the advice, 'Sleep on it.' On the upside, wakefulness allows your imagination to bypass reality. In the dawn of the restless night, I sometimes rewrite my mother's story. It ends in a cosy cottage overlooking Dartmoor: she's seventy-three and happily married to her third husband, an antique dealer with a quaint little shop in Totnes; she has a golden retriever named Sparky and a lovingly tended garden in bloom. Best of all, her latest romantic novel has just been published to glowing reviews. As with most fantasies, it could never have happened; even Sparky is out of place since I recently discovered she was scared of dogs.

So many things provoke thoughts of my mother, some direct, others oblique. Listening to Radio 4 shortly before it hands over to the World Service, I think of her when I hear 'Sailing By', the piece of music that introduces the *Shipping Forecast*. It's a buoyant tune heralding life-saving information. There's enchantment in the names of the isolated coastal stations — Viking, Forties, German Bight and my favourite, Scilly Automatic — but it's in the storm warnings that I hear a message for my mother: in the harshest of conditions a station is said to be 'losing its identity'. For now, she was as remote to me as Faeroes or Fastnet 'falling slowly'.

8

The (not so) Grand Tour

During one particularly troubled and impecunious period after he made his escape from
Castle Greyskull in 1977, my cousin David
ended up homeless and sleeping in a car.
Back at the Castle, it seems Gomez assumed
I would take on David's role. I never won a
single argument, but I stood my ground and
tried to answer back. At sixteen, I didn't have
much of an armoury but I gave it my best
shot, though I wish I'd known about the
withering look my father fired at the Housey
bullies.

According to Gomez, I was disrespectful,
insolent and ungrateful, but it was my
defiance that wound him up most. The more
irate Gomez grew, the higher his pitch would
climb, until he sounded like a cross between
Basil Fawlty and Mickey Mouse. On the one
hand it was hard to take him seriously, but
the simmering wrath was almost worse than
the eruption, which could be set off by a wet
towel left on the bathroom floor, the
dish-washing not up to clinical standard or

even a misconstrued anecdote, but most frequently by any opinion that opposed his. Incensed by the trivial and enraged by the political, his dogmatism left me perplexed and embarrassed: pro-vivisection and anti-euthanasia, down with socialism and bleeding heart liberals, and don't get him started on the Irish. There was no debate and no conferring, Gomez was the only person whose opinion was never wrong. Funny that. His grandfather, Even the borderline Commie, would have hung his head in shame.

The fights alternated with huffy sulking, both his and mine; having been too delicate for rugby at school, Gomez sulked for Wales. The atmosphere around the dinner table was as grim and silent as ever. After about six months I chose to cook for myself and ate my cheese on toast and spaghetti hoops in my room.

At Camden School for Girls discipline was non-existent and homework easily avoided. Compared to Christ's Hospital, it was more like a day centre for truants and I spent most of my time with the other skivers in the sixth-form smoking room. I had no chance of passing my exams and left school halfway through A-levels.

I'd scraped five Cs at O-level, and with no

discernible skills, I found a job as a cocktail waitress at a nightclub in Mayfair. At seventeen, I was under age but it was the least of the club's illegalities. It was a sleazy dive with sticky floors and dodgy deals at every table, its clientele wide-boys and felons, rich men in suits and girls on the make. I was propositioned nightly but learned pretty quick how to take care of myself: with an ingenuous smile and a fabricated house rule, I side-stepped offers of cocaine and invitations for late suppers at the Hilton or the Connaught. It was an early introduction to the seedier side of life and I could spot a lowlife at twenty paces. After a taxi home and a take-away at 3 a.m., I slept till noon. One of the benefits of working nights was that I rarely saw Morticia and Gomez.

On my nights off my social life was typically teenage: gigs at the Marquee, the Roundhouse and the Hope and Anchor in Islington, with an unsuitable collection of boyfriends. One was an actor-bartender twice my age, another a dissolute drummer with a gambling habit; it seems my taste in men was as misjudged as my mother's. There was, however, the steadying influence of my school friend Claudia's parents, with weekends at their cottage in the country and dinners at Acacia Road, up the hill yet a million miles from Castle Greyskull. That year, I spent the first of many Christmases with my surrogate family, Morticia and Gomez having absented themselves to Marbella again.

I wasn't a bad girl as such, my blunders and misdemeanours more naïve than heinous. Over dinner one evening, in an attempt to break the Trappist hush, I recounted what I thought was a mildly amusing story. Earlier that day at Paddington Station, I'd helped a little old lady and her heavy luggage on to a train as it was leaving the platform — how was I to know she didn't speak English and had been struggling to get *off* the train? Gomez didn't find it at all funny and I got a rollocking for not establishing the facts. After that I kept my anecdotes to myself and was inevitably told off for being so secretive.

I wasn't doing drugs, or shop-lifting or vandalising phone boxes, but my most errant offence almost earned me a criminal record. One weekend, my friend Ally and I went down to Brighton to see the punk band the Stranglers. Having attracted the attention of one of their roadies, we were invited backstage and ended up having dinner with the band at their hotel at about 2 a.m. It ought to have been a thrilling escapade for a couple of faux punk teenagers. However, it was about to assume the shape of a pear.

One of the Stranglers' entourage had been arrested for possession, and we all piled into the band's van to 'rescue' him. When we got to the police station, a scuffle rather than a punch-up developed between the punks and the uniforms, resulting in all of us spending the night at Her Majesty's pleasure. We were released the next morning, and Ally and I were charged with being drunk and disorderly and obstructing a policeman in his duty. Drunk on two beers? I don't think so. As for obstruction, well, we were in the vicinity of the scuffle. I wouldn't have minded quite so much if the *Evening Standard*, which reported the incident, had mentioned our names.

Morticia and Gomez were abroad again at the time, and Sue, who was temping for Gomez at his office, accepted the first of many guardian angel missions. She called them in Los Angeles and broke the news with tact and diplomacy, thereby preventing an international incident. Ally and I were acquitted at a hearing two months later, but my copybook was seriously blotted.

Whichever way I played it, I didn't fit into the neatly arranged and nicely beige environment at Castle Greyskull. The Rubicon was crossed when I stayed out all weekend at a boyfriend's flat. I didn't let Morticia and

Gomez know where I was because I thought they wouldn't notice my empty bedroom. When I got back on Monday I found a note telling me to call the office. Ten minutes later Gomez stormed through the door. He was incoherent with rage, arms flailing and his finger jabbing in my face. It was one-sided combat and I don't think I managed even one complete sentence in my defence. Purple-faced and spitting, the last thing he squeaked was, 'Pack your bags and get out!' He told me I couldn't stay at Grandma's, which as he well knew left me with few options, or perhaps he was hoping I had nowhere to go. Morticia stood behind him and did nothing.

I was no doubt as incoherent as he was, and as close to hysterical sobbing as I ever want to be, much as I hated letting Gomez see me cry. I packed my clothes and a few books into carrier bags. It was mid February, two months after my eighteenth birthday, and to complete the scene, it was below freezing and snowing. I had about £3 to my name and couldn't afford a taxi. I called my guardian angel Sue, who was the only person I knew with a car. Hearing the desperation in my voice on the phone she was at the door within twenty minutes. As the four of us stood in the hallway, Gomez hurled another tirade at Sue for helping me, to say nothing of her disloyalty as a member of his staff. Ten years older and wiser than me, she knew all about the withering look and delivered it like a pro.

Sue drove me and my meagre belongings to Claudia's house in St John's Wood. I was a child in need of a home and her parents, Klaus and Ursula, took me in without question. Over the years, they've done the same for many of their two daughters' friends; whether dispossessed or between lodgings, at Acacia Road we were family. Ursula put an extra blanket on the bed in the spare room and made me a cup of cocoa.

I didn't hear from Morticia and Gomez for about three months. After that, a formal but impervious channel was opened, but I saw them as little as possible. The eviction was never mentioned again. I wasn't sure why but I kept it secret for nearly two decades, and aside from Sue and Claudia, not even my closest friends knew that my uncle had kicked me out on the street. In the years since, a recurring question flickered at the back of my mind: What would my mother have thought?

Certain moments in life bring a breath-taking clarity. One such Damascene instant occurred eight years ago as Claudia and I were settling into our seats at the theatre. 'I've never told you this,' she said, 'but about two days after you came to live with us, Gomez called my mum and said, 'Tell Anna to put the keys through the door, and that she's not welcome here.'' He didn't ask whether I was okay, nor did he thank Claudia's mother for taking me in. As the house lights went down I felt the blood drain from my face, leaving me cold with shame and anger.

My mind in a turmoil of ugly memories, I remember nothing of the performance on stage as I thought of my cousin David curled up under a blanket in the back of a car, the rigid formality at Castle Greyskull and the grim Christmas dinners I'd felt obliged to attend and, most of all, the hypocrisy of Gomez saying, 'We think of you as our daughter.' In loco parentis indeed. As the curtain came down for the interval, I drew the line.

That December Morticia sent a card that said, 'I hope we'll see you on Christmas Day.' She enclosed a cheque for £250. I was about to have spinal surgery again and badly needed the money, but I would rather have starved than cash it. I returned the cheque with a note declining their hospitality. That was in 1997 and I haven't heard from Morticia and Gomez since. If it were anyone else I'd put their silence down to a guilty conscience.

When Sue and I recently talked through the motive behind my eviction from the first

Castle Greyskull, she said, 'Gomez wanted to teach you a lesson and was hopping mad because you had friends to turn to. I honestly think he wanted to cast you out on to the street so you'd *really* learn your lesson.' When she said he never forgave her for rescuing me and taking my side, it reminded me of Grandma and her intractable need to divide the family into those who were for and against her.

It's also possible he was bluffing when he told me to pack my bags; perhaps he thought I would promise to behave and beg to be allowed to stay. No chance! For one thing my pride would have prevented it. 'When it became obvious that you were never going to kowtow, you had to be punished for it,' Sue went on. 'And when you stayed out all weekend, you gave him the perfect excuse. With Gomez, you were always in the wrong — end of story.'

★　★　★

I spent the next few years on a rudderless yet independent odyssey, having cut myself free of both Gomez and Grandma's influence. Eventually, at twenty-one, I drifted as far as New York, which proved the best place for me. In stark contrast to my aimlessness, it was at around the same age that my father's career took off, together with his love life. The brief flings of his late teens evolved into short-lived affairs. Many of his girlfriends were older than him; they were also in various ways unattainable, and included, it was rumoured, the ballerinas Andrée Howard and Diana Gould (later Lady Menuhin), both more than ten years his senior. Easily enchanted and easily bruised, his defence strategy was to replace one infatuation with another.

His BBC colleague Terence Cooper observed these liaisons with bemusement and concern. Now a sprightly ninety-three, Terence was twelve years older than my father, a level-headed friend who noted a pattern of behaviour: 'Michael was often unhappy over some girl, until she returned his affections, then he'd lose interest. It may have been immaturity, but I think it was the pursuit rather than the prize that fired him.' Terence was paraphrasing Henry James in an essay titled 'The Art of Fiction', though it wasn't quite what the Master intended when he wrote: 'Be generous and delicate and pursue the prize.' The architect and thriller writer Stephen Gardiner interpreted these pursuits as driven by my father's fear of losing his freedom: 'Michael struck me as sensible and clear-sighted but I found his restlessness with women a little disturbing.'

Terence and Stephen, like so many others, remember my father as a complex and ambiguous character who wore different faces with different people. By turns playful and introspective, few were allowed to see, let alone stroke the black dog sniffing at his heels. Terence caught only glimpses of my father's depression, while Stephen saw him as the promising young writer with a weakness for pretty girls. Whichever face my father wore, it was presented in semi-profile.

As soon as the borders reopened after the war, those who could scrape the money together left for abroad. Many wrote the book that marked a rite of passage, but only for the talented few was it the transition from writer to author. My father began his career proper with *Ilex and Olive*, an account of his travels through France and Italy. Entrenched in the past and the Europe of the eighteenth-century Grand Tour, he wrote: 'I am forced to admit I am an escapist, a sentimentalist unable to live completely in the world of my time.'

He arrived in Paris on the evening of 25 August 1946, the second anniversary of the Liberation. The city was floodlit and the streets packed with cheering crowds waving tricolor flags. In drab and joyless London ruined buildings and shortages of every kind made sure its citizens had little to celebrate. In Paris there was rationing but no bombsites, the Nazis having entered the capital unopposed by the fleeing French government, thus guaranteeing the preservation of Notre Dame, the Opéra and the Palais Royal.

In part an extended essay on art and architecture, *Ilex and Olive* is peppered with amorous interludes, which inadvertently reveal more about my father than his appreciation of rococo elegance and Palladian symmetry. His tone is self-effacing throughout and the book opens with him wining and dining a showgirl in a seedy Place Pigalle nightclub. After several drinks and the promise of a taxi back to her place, she disappears through an emergency exit. Stuck with an astronomical champagne bill, he'd fallen for the city's oldest scam: 'My first night in Paris and I was already an English sucker.'

En route to the south he leaves a succession of farewells in his wake, from the neurotic expat to the local seamstress's daughter. He lays bare their hidden natures by gesture as much as dialogue. At a bar on the harbour front in Cap Ferrat, he sits at a corner table with a beer and a cigarette, listening as a faded blonde entertains a group of young soldiers. Her French is fluent but slurred, and 'she has the rather rounded back of someone accustomed to spending the most interesting part of her life on a bar stool. Yet beneath her tawdry sophistication one could see glimpses, like a partly exposed palimpsest, of a life she had lived before this.' She buys another round of drinks and signals for my father to join them. Sensing he's about to be led astray, he names the woman Eve.

> 'Thank God,' she says, 'someone I can talk English to,' and dismisses her coterie, promising to meet them the following evening. Eve was rather drunk by now. 'I'm mean sometimes,' she says. 'Weak and mean. Have a drink with me.' She was a talker. Every smallest matter connected with herself she found of enormous interest — and so did I.

A barfly with a thousand tales to tell, Eve is in her mid thirties, a divorcee with a county accent and a hefty alimony cheque, who can well afford the rounds of drinks she so freely buys. She's staying at the local hotel but invites him back to the villa she's renting, claiming she's afraid to sleep there alone.

175

Ensconced on the sofa and poised for seduction:

The light from the table lamp, whether by accident or design, smoothed away the lines on her face. I moved closer to her. I was more than a little drunk and now she seemed beautiful. Her lips were about six inches from mine when, with a sudden acceleration, she gave me a quick kiss and jumped to her feet. 'I must get back to my hotel,' she said. 'Don't come with me. There are eyes at every window.'

A lonely and paranoid tease, Eve buys talking time with aperitifs and the promise of sex. Bewildered and frustrated, my father retires to his bedroom.

Late the following morning as he sunbathes on the terrace, she returns to the villa, hung over and bad-tempered. In the cold light of day the now sober young man passes judgement:

Like many women upon whom the maturer charm is gradually descending she wore dark glasses. She was evidently proud of her legs; she sat on a deckchair and extended them to brown in the sun, then she removed her glasses. The sun glared on her heavily made-up face, and I realised, to my horror, that I could see no attraction in her whatever. My image of beauty was utterly destroyed.

Following their thwarted one-night stand Eve and my father are eager to part. He returns to his hotel, relieved but undaunted; there was always Paris.

Back in the capital, 'the year is dimming, the return to London near. Paris receives, but does not satisfy; she offers and suggests all manner of delectation and reward which she will never give.' He associates the city with a woman he refers to only as 'C.'. She taunts him, their relationship yet to be consummated:

Last night I left her vowing I would not see her again, and today I have walked till my heels are blistered. A message from her asks me to ring. No, I will not. But at seven I rang her, weakly, hating myself, yet aching to see her, to be tortured once more for another evening. I prepare myself for a night of nervous turning and feverish imaginings.

'C.' was Catherine Macmillan, the future Prime Minister's daughter. Born into a privileged family cursed on both sides, from the maternal Cavendish line (her grandfather was the Duke of Devonshire) she inherited chronic alcoholism and from the Macmillans clinical depression, legacies that compelled her to crash through the conservative barricade.

Rapacious and sexually uninhibited, Catherine was both sadist and masochist, and she tormented my father until she got what she wanted. According to his friend Francis King, my father eventually obliged, but reluctantly: 'He told me she liked to be beaten, but it wasn't his kind of thing.' Catherine had no control over her drinking, but in the S & M set-up the submissive is in charge.

Catherine and my father were motivated by pain of a different kind. Writing to Maurice Cranston, one of his closest friends, he confessed: 'I find myself thinking about her every moment of the day, furious, humiliated but still hopelessly in love. I must be the most asinine masochist to put up with her treatment.' Despite his protests, he found perverse pleasure in love's torment: the rose with the sharpest thorns offers the sweetest perfume, but Catherine extracted the perfume for herself and left him with nothing but wilting petals. My father's niece Sheila, who was about seventeen at the time, recalls him confiding in her: 'He was besotted with Catherine. I was rather embarrassed and confused when he said she was very demanding in bed but he thought she was a lesbian. Innocent that I was, I went home that evening and told my mother, 'Michael's new girlfriend is a Wesleyan.''

The unauthorised biography *The Macmillans* by Richard Davenport-Hines contains a photograph of Catherine taken in her early twenties. She's dressed in a winter coat with one button casually done up and a silk scarf thrown around her neck. At first glance she looks almost plain, but the longer I studied her face the more beautiful she became. Her expression is knowing yet childlike, challenging the camera with the smile of a deviant angel. I can see why so many men fell under her bad girl spell. Peregrine Worsthorne was also briefly in thrall to Catherine. When I told him my father had proposed to her, he smiled and said, 'So did I. So did we all.'

My father was twenty-three when he met Catherine. She was twenty, but already knew how to inflict pain with precision. He was fit and strong, but his one physical defect not only prevented him from joining up when his friends went off to war, it also undermined his masculinity. He was unable to see that an imperfection can also work as a Byronic asset. Catherine apparently couldn't see it either.

Paris was the perfect setting for my father's proposal, its broad boulevards and arched bridges instilled with the romantic heritage of the nineteenth century. His feelings for the city of lovers were ambivalent, yet he was intoxicated by the sentiments of Hugo and Zola and their evocation of sufferings beyond endurance and the insights only despair can bring. He must have spent the day in nervous anticipation, rehearsing his line and patting the pocket that held the tiny velvet-lined box. Over dessert at a restaurant on the Left Bank, he presented Catherine with the ring. There was no gasp of surprise or delight. Instead, with unconcealed laughter, she said, 'I couldn't possibly marry a man with a glass eye.'

He didn't mention the incident in *Ilex and Olive*, but wrote in his Postscript, 'Paris: since that last embarrassing apostrophe to an ideal I have not touched this journal.' Catherine fitted his ideal in that she was unattainable, and though he might have steeled himself to hear that she couldn't possibly marry an impoverished writer, I doubt he anticipated such a wounding rejection.

Perry Worsthorne said she would have been better off with either of them than the man she did marry, the Tory MP Julian Amery. In later life her masochism would be fully gratified. Richard Davenport-Hines told me she became decrepit through alcoholism and osteoporosis, and was by turns pathetic, aggressive, self-pitying and bitter: 'Her husband was also a heavy drinker and a vain, upper-class flirt with a roving eye. There were many affairs on both sides, but the marriage lasted because Julian depended on the Macmillan trust fund.'

In a picture taken about twenty years after the 'deviant angel' photograph, Catherine's eyes are downcast and the corners of her mouth puckered and sour. Her hair is neatly tied back, but beneath her buttoned-up coat she's a woman in disarray. Towards the end of her life she was in constant pain from two collapsed vertebrae, but still drinking steadily and smoking forty cigarettes a day. Woodrow Wyatt, another former lover, wrote in his *Journals* shortly before her death: 'I remember that beautiful girl from 1949, perhaps the most beautiful girl in London. [Now] She was covered with sores, her face blotched in a hideous way . . . and she smelled a bit of pee.' Catherine died in 1991 at the age of sixty-five, a neglected wife, physical wreck and bloated alcoholic. It was a terrible and humiliating end, but when I think of her cruelty to my father it makes me want to quote Wittgenstein: 'The human body is the best picture of the human soul.'

Women such as Catherine and Eve betrayed their own vulnerabilities as well as my father's. I wonder who he was looking for in all these unsuitable sirens. The answer might lie in his preoccupation with Henry James and his recurring themes of unrequited love, emotional repression and the erotic anonymity of the displaced traveller. Unavailability and a fascination with aristocratic women provided a safety net, or alibi, for both authors but for very different reasons. For James, sex was a messy business best avoided by writing; for my father, *love* was a messy business best avoided by sex.

In *The Aspern Papers*, James wrote: 'That most fatal of human passions, our not knowing when to stop'. When my father fell in love he didn't know where to draw the line. Poised and in control professionally, when it came to intimate relationships he was incapable of exerting the same discipline. When I asked Elizabeth Rosenberg — a close friend and an editor at Longman's — for her immediate impressions of my father, she said, 'He was very ambitious, one was always aware of that. And, of course, he was a womaniser, but he had an air of insecurity around women. There was something of the masquerade about him.'

★   ★   ★

In his Prologue he wrote that his journey on the page was disjointed: 'The only unity is the trickling line from Dieppe to Capri, and its only form is that it is formless.' He also admitted that he remained *dégagé*, as if he needed to keep a safe distance between himself and the reader. *Ilex and Olive* was published in 1949, and the reviews were positive if reserved. The *TLS* said: 'Mr Swan displays an enviable gift in the comparative assessment of varieties of painters, sculptors and architects. [Yet] the shape of the book suffers from them and the joins show.' The most intuitive was Naomi Lewis in the *New Statesman*: 'Mr Swan tries on one mask and then another . . . and shows both the attraction and the restlessness.'

My father's female friends were acutely aware of this mask, and none more so than Iliana Cranston (*née* Baroness Maximiliana von Fraunberg). They met at the Italian Embassy in London in the late 1940s. 'Michael was a kind and sensitive soul but he seemed to have a compulsion with women,' Iliana said. 'He seemed to be caught up in the

183

macho attitude of that time and the need to take charge.' As sensitive as he was, he was also unable to turn down an opportunity.

'He knew I was in love with someone else, but he made a half-hearted pass at me one evening when he was staying with my family in Florence,' Iliana said. 'I turned him down gently and he looked almost relieved. The following morning I asked him why he'd pounced on me and he said, 'Because I felt I should.'' The macho attitude once again masked his true feelings.

Not long after we met in 2002, Iliana gave me a cache of twelve letters from my father. His voice was friendly and inquisitive as he talked of his travels, his mild anxiety over the imminent publication of his latest book and news of friends and family, but one letter, posted in Rome, was of an entirely different tone:

Darling, you never let me tell you what's slowly been gathering in my heart. You force me to write in cold words the things I long to tell you. I've loved you in this quiet way as a friend always. But now it's so far from the same. I no longer simply love you but am in love with you. Darling Iliana, I write this letter so that you shall know that when I tried to take you in my arms it was a clumsy symbol of my love for you — not, a thousand times not, a frivolous, meaningless act. It's a love whose purity almost confounds me; I've been an old lecher for so long that this sudden sense of love without the slightest trace of lust brings flushes to my cheeks. Trust me darling. With love, Michael.

His words brought flushes to my cheeks too, and I felt like an eavesdropper outside the confessional. It's always safer to write from the heart than to speak from it, a negative response by mail less crushing than a rejection in person. It was probably an easy letter to compose but a hard one to drop into the postbox. I imagined him standing on a Roman street corner hovering outside the post office both longing for and dreading his letter's reception. I felt the jolt in his stomach as he let go of the small brown envelope.

Over the telephone I read Iliana my father's letter, my voice faltering at certain phrases. 'Oh, my dear,' she said. 'I'd forgotten his passion.' His plea was indeed passionate, but in writing of a 'purity' that almost confounds him he severs love from lust as if the two were in conflict. Lust was easy and made few demands, but for my father love was far more complicated: when tarnished with sexual desire it became degraded.

Aside from his dignity, he risked little in sending his letter since he knew Iliana was already spoken for. It was a young man's passing infatuation and the dream remained intact; unrequited love had its benefits. Happily, his confession didn't damage their friendship. 'I can't recall what I wrote in response,' Iliana said, 'but Michael was very precious to me and I wouldn't have jeopardised our friendship for anything.' Enclosed with the letter was a photograph taken at the Opera House in Florence, my father in a pin-striped suit and Iliana in a chiffon gown and fur wrap, a sparkly evening bag clutched in her elegant hands. It's no wonder he was infatuated, she looks like a movie star.

Iliana was the Jamesian archetype, a blonde and beguiling baroness just out of reach. In the second of his books on Henry James, published in 1952, two years before his declaration of love, his dedication reads: 'For Iliana von Fraunberg. 'In life there are two paths open to you: one leads to the ideal, the other to death.''

The quotation is from Friedrich Schiller's 1796 poem *The Ideal Freedom*. Taken out of time and context, such idealism imposes its own kind of tyranny; for my father Schiller's two paths led to the same place. I can't help thinking this black and white view was the source of his despair, and it makes me want to sit him down and tell him that life is shaded in grey, rough around the edges and, more often than not, gloriously messy.

For the time being, the Jamesian alibi served my father well, at home and abroad. Marigold Hunt (now married to the historian and *Spectator* columnist Paul Johnson) had a six-month affair with my father in 1954. She was twenty-two and he was thirty-one, and neither had any false illusions: 'He was delightful company but a little detached emotionally. For some reason, we were both discreet about the affair. I remember the excitement of knowing I was a secret person in his life, as if he needed to keep me in a compartment.' Like Iliana, Marigold fell into the 'purity' category: 'My mind has carefully screened out whether we actually slept together or not, but I think we didn't. There was no feeling of lust from Michael, though he was very affectionate and a good kisser.'

For my father, it seems there were only good girls and bad girls; perhaps the wordsmith in him saw that lust is an anagram of slut. The division separating the women he idealised and the girls he lusted after was unbreachable; but between purity and promiscuity there lay a wealth of opportunity.

As a freelance writer he was committed to no one, except his editors. As a single young man his libido told him who was a threat to his liberty and who wasn't. For Marigold it was far less complicated, a brief but sweet interlude that ended amicably: 'I knew the relationship wasn't going anywhere, and when he went to Mexico for six months it just fizzled out.' Not only was travel his calling it was also his 'get-out' clause, though Marigold suspected another motive.

Despite my father's reputation as a lothario, she was convinced he was hiding other secret compartments: 'We all believed there were men in his life, and I thought that was why our affair was rather ineffectual.' Nearly all his friends, including Stephen Gardiner, assumed he was bisexual: 'There was nothing camp about Michael, but I did wonder if all those girls were a cover.'

He may have extricated himself from Housey's homoerotic atmosphere, but as a shrewd young man he was at ease in the company of gay friends such as Somerset Maugham, Angus Wilson, Harold Acton, John Lehmann and J.R. Ackerley, perhaps because there were no sexual expectations, at least on his part. My father was a born flirt and knew how to capitalise on his looks. In 1947, during a second research trip for *Ilex and Olive*, he spent the summer working for Somerset Maugham at the Villa Mauresque in Cap Ferrat. My father was twenty-four and Maugham, known to his friends as Willy, seventy-three. He did his own typing and my father's role was more decorative than secretarial.

He described the early morning ritual at the Villa Mauresque: Maugham would appear with a white towel around his waist, and after a few yoga exercises he plunged into the sea, accompanied by my father. His friend Raleigh Trevelyan confirms the story: 'Michael told me that after their swim Willy liked to watch him sunbathe. One morning he said, 'With a body like yours you can go anywhere.' For Michael, it was a case of look but don't touch.'

My father wrote that Maugham was 'unfailingly courteous but given to sudden bursts of rage which soon pass; he is as capable of violent prejudice as he is of the most generous thought and action.' He knew how to flatter and cajole even the prickliest of characters, and learned a lot from Maugham during his brief internship, most notably the value of restraint: 'He went no further than the bare recounting of an incident, offering no comment beyond what was inherent in his words, presenting you with the facts and leaving you to make up your own mind . . . the restless observer standing in infinite alcoves watching the peculiar antics of humanity.'

Maugham was an observer and my father a listener. A natural mimic and verbal magpie, he often stole cadence and intonation for future reference: 'Maugham speaks in an even, unhurried tempo with a rather musical effect. I wondered whether this perfect control of pitch and tempo might not have been the result of his victory over his stammer.' His impression of Maugham's faltering delivery would later feature in his repertoire.

The writer and aesthete Harold Acton was equally imitable. Francis King described his genteel modulations as 'fluting upwards and then sliding downwards, in the manner of Edith Evans'. Seasoned gossip that he was, Acton reportedly said of my father and Francis during the time they shared a villa in Florence later that summer, 'Some say they do, some say they don't. But two such attractive young men . . . all alone in that villa . . . *I* say they do.' They didn't, but my father neither admitted nor denied the rumours.

'I'm sure Michael was highly amused that

we all thought he was bisexual,' Perry Worsthorne said. 'He was such an inscrutable character and I can see him standing to one side at parties with a mysterious smile on his face . . . I think he liked to keep people guessing.' Secure in his heterosexuality, if not his masculinity, he enjoyed playing with other people's curiosity.

★   ★   ★

My father left home at the end of 1946 and moved into a studio flat in the red-light enclave of Shepherd Market. Concealed by a covered walkway and in need of a lick of paint, the network of narrow streets and alleyways remains a hidden and slightly tatty pocket out of place in smartly dressed Mayfair.

In spite of its dubious reputation Shepherd Market was a friendly village in the heart of the city. Horse-drawn carts still made early morning deliveries: fish from Billingsgate and flowers from Covent Garden, as well as huge blocks of ice for the catering trade. Outside the French bistro, melting ice trickled across the flagstones to my father's front door.

I often picture him working at a rickety desk in his first-floor flat above the Express Dairy. Shivering in the chill air, he's wearing a scarf and an extra jumper as he can't afford the coal to light the fire. In the street below his window the prostitutes, gussied up in their fox furs and ankle chains, are bickering over a stolen pitch. Filtering out their caterwauling he lights another cigarette, his fountain pen rarely leaving the page.

Except for the chemist and newsagent, the traditional establishments are long gone, but there's still the odd knocking shop among the cafés and galleries. Next to my father's building, a dimly lit hallway alerts passers-by to a handwritten sign reading 'Busty Model'. Shepherd Market is holding on to its heritage by a bra strap.

Number 32 is a tall, skinny building over a vacant shop and I could just make out the faded Express Dairy sign. I was determined to see my father's home during his most productive and happiest period. Whenever I was in the area I rang all three doorbells but with no reply. After about eighteen months, I finally tracked down the landlord, Robin Stephenson.

Robin led me up the doll's house staircase to the first floor. The patterned carpet was the colour of old age; it was probably the same carpet my father had trudged up, the rain and snow on the soles of his shoes contributing to its murkiness. The bed-sitting room was lit by a bare light bulb hanging from a chipped plaster rose. The original fireplace was still there, sea-green tiles and black slate surround. I'd thought I would sense my father there, working at his desk by the window, but the only presence I felt was that of a different tenant.

Uncle John told me that their mother had sublet the flat during one of my father's research trips, to a very nice girl who was well spoken and expensively dressed. 'When Michael came back six months later, she refused to leave,' John said. 'One evening we sat in the bistro opposite and waited for her to go out. We changed the locks, packed up her things and left them in the hallway.' Among her belongings they found photographic evidence that this nice girl had been entertaining clients, dressed up in a variety of outfits from schoolboy to dominatrix. 'In one photo,' John recounted with evident glee, 'she was standing, whip in hand, over a naked man in a studded collar eating out of a dog bowl.'

When I visited, the tenants, respectable or otherwise, were long gone. The flat had been empty for a year and smelled stale and musty. The decaying veil of a net curtain hid a grimy window and the tiny kitchen and bathroom were coated in a fine layer of dust: the rooms appeared forsaken and reluctant to let go of the past. All trace of bustling productivity had vanished, leaving a mouldering chill in the air. I got there just in time: Robin told me the builders would start work in a few weeks, gutting it to convert the three flats into a luxury apartment. I was there only for about fifteen minutes, but for days after when I put on my coat I caught the whiff of damp trapped in its fibres.

★ ★ ★

Topsy lived to see his son's first book published, in March 1949. Topsy's career had picked up after he placed an advertisement in *The Times*, but he was working with a heavy heart. Nearly all his commissions were from the relatives of servicemen who had died during the war. He was painting from photographs, and nowhere was his lighting more ghostly as he portrayed the spirits of young men in uniform. Among the letters from their families was one from the Drapers Company informing him that he was on the short list to execute a portrait of George VI. Around this time Topsy was diagnosed with prostate cancer. Towards the end he was in and out of hospital but he wanted to die at home. Uncle John was by then a GP and felt it his duty to help his father as he had the fatally wounded soldiers in his care. When the pain became unbearable, he gave Topsy a lethal injection of morphine. It was one of his most compassionate acts.

During his last days Topsy would have found comfort in my father's success; perhaps in some way his dignified death was made a little easier by knowing that his son was a published author. In a very different way my relationship with my father has also been determined by his writing.

★　★　★

With my maternal family's encouragement I grew up disliking my father and detached myself from him in every way possible. His titles on the bookshelf represented his presence, which I tried to ignore; his absence was much easier to deal with. During my teens I would occasionally open one of his books, read a paragraph or two, then slam it shut. I didn't want to like anything about him, but I found his observations touching and funny. He writes of a Carib couple who befriend him in Guyana: 'William treated his shy, almost silent wife with undemonstrative love, and when we camped he would sling their hammock some distance from the others. As soon as we had eaten they would retire to their carapace, murmuring affectionately together until they fell asleep.' And of a tribe in the Guyana interior: 'Akawaios in particular have an intense curiosity about all forms of experience. I was told of one who paddled for a month down to Bartica because a friend had told him of a prostitute there whose genitalia were of unique construction.' It disturbed me that my father could make me laugh.

It wasn't until I started writing that I read his books from cover to cover — only to find that he was even more of a mystery. I couldn't connect the isolated, angry giant of my childhood with the sensitive, enquiring traveller. Now that I've spent time with my father through his work and his friends I've met an entirely different man, and I'm surprised how much I like him.

I first met his friend Stephen Gardiner at one of Francis King's book launches. When I introduced myself Stephen looked at me with a puzzled expression, as if transported back in time. Halfway through a sentence he paused and smiled. 'How extraordinary,' he said. 'I thought I recognised you when you walked through the door, but now that I'm talking to you I can see a trace of your father. You tilt your head to one side when you're listening, just like Michael.' It was a mannerism I was unaware of until Stephen pointed it out. Other than a passion for words, I'd always thought my father and I had little in common. It was my first experience of our shared physicality, and I rather liked it. As my coolness towards him thaws I'm finally learning to appreciate the similarities as well as the differences.

'I was quite envious of your father,' Perry Worsthorne told me. 'He was much talked about as one of the best young writers of the time.' Alongside his books and broadcasts, my father wrote scores of essays and articles for journals such as the *New Statesman*, *Punch* and the *Spectator*. He reviewed novels by Evelyn Waugh, Kingsley Amis and V.S. Naipaul, and analysed subjects as diverse as flamenco, Renaissance painting and modern printing, all the while casually dropping references to Plato and Seneca, Mithraism and monotheism.

My father's style was the written equivalent of Received Pronunciation and his bible, *Fowler's Use of English*: God forbid one should split an infinitive or end a sentence with a preposition. It was heavily punctuated, as much with semicolons as rarefied terms *amour propre, démodé, romantisch, gemütlich, mutatis mutandis* among others, or, as my father would have written, *inter alia*. Affected as those italics seem now, in his day they were almost mandatory, as if plain English were unacceptably lowbrow. I admire his erudition and covet his cultural frame of reference but his style feels constricted and mannered. I prefer him when he's less 'writerly', coining spontaneous impressions such as, 'The moon had let herself be party to a confidence trick' and 'the ragged shoeless beggars who appear silently at your café table like some Eumenides without the upper hand'. His books were ultimately destined for a limited readership and I can't imagine him writing, or wanting to write, bestsellers. I think he wrote to please himself but made sure he sold enough copies to secure his next contract.

The economics of the literary life were precarious and one of the reasons my father was so prolific: the need to pay the bills focused his mind. A practice common among freelancers was to collect a dozen or so new titles from the relevant editor at various journals and newspapers, decide which ones to review and sell the remainder, in my father's case to his friend Handyside Buchanan, proprietor of the Heywood Hill bookshop on Curzon Street, round the corner from Shepherd Market.

As for his social and professional commitments, he saw no need to step outside his caste. All his friends were in publishing or the arts; there were no lawyers, engineers or accountants in his circle. In the 1950s, literary London was in many ways a closed shop, and it was pedigree rather than privilege that invited admission; as left-leaning and liberal-minded as its denizens were, the correct accent counted.

My father fitted the profile: public school, patrician antecedents and a bank account in the red. He was also a charming, cordial and sought-after guest at the intimate at-home salons where, Francis King says, 'Michael knew how to sing for his supper. He was terrifically entertaining and a wonderful mimic. One of his best party-pieces was his stuttering Somerset Maugham.'

My father's friend Tony Curtis describes his unusual combination of modesty and aplomb: 'He was a regular at all the parties, but he wasn't a name-dropper and was never pushy. Nor did he boast about his work. Michael was always more interested in hearing about his friends' books than talking about his own. Coupled with his attentive and equable manner and the gift of getting people to unburden themselves, he was enormously appealing to women.'

As for my father's peripatetic love life, Tony provides a convincing explanation: 'I sensed there was a conflict in Michael between living the literary life to the full or settling down and getting married. It was the classic dilemma of the man of letters with no private income. In those days men paid for everything, and Michael simply couldn't afford a long-term girlfriend.' Wedded to his career, at this time only one woman threatened his fidelity.

My father invested so much in his career there was little left over for anything more than passing infatuations. The bachelor life suited him yet he was in awe of the elusive grand passion. As an idealist he couldn't see beyond the fulfilment of the dream, but in his search for the flawless and the sparkling he overlooked the value of durability; his was a champagne fantasy devoid of domesticity, its sentiments embodied in contemporary Valentine's Day clichés. For the dreamer, weekends in Paris and Venice or fine wine and red roses eclipse the shared considerations real love brings — the laundry, the dishes in the sink and grocery shopping at Waitrose. For the realist, there's as much romance in the fruit and veg aisle as there is in strolling hand in hand across the moonlit Bridge of Sighs.

Until the age of thirty-two his writing came

first. It was 1955, the year of the Warsaw Pact alliance, the polio vaccine and a new Tory Prime Minister, the highly strung Anthony Eden, as yet unaware of the chaos the following year would bring with Suez and the Hungarian Uprising. Lonnie Donegan and his skifflemen strummed their tea chests and washboards at the 100 Club and the 606, and everyone was whistling the theme tune to *The Dam Busters*. The middle year of the decade also saw a dramatic shift in social conscience when Ruth Ellis was the last woman in Britain to be hanged.

At home history was unfolding and times slowly changing, but for my father elsewhere was always a happier place. He voted Labour but showed little interest in politics. By now he was far more intrigued by the economics and culture of Central and South America. His fourth book, *Temples of the Sun and Moon*, was published to critical acclaim. *The Times* noted: 'Mr Swan has forged a literary style, clear, flowing and direct . . . this is a book that broadens our knowledge of Mexico and its peoples, and in a quiet, unpretentious way, also reaches the broader horizons of universal experience.' Harold Nicolson wrote in the *Observer*: 'Mr Swan has rendered his prose beautifully. The problem of combining unity of impression with variety of experience could not have been more perfectly solved.' Compared to the reticent criticism of his first book, he was now earning the kind of reviews authors could only long for.

'Gold is a tricky, dangerous thing . . . no sooner had the dream been formed than the gold was no more. El Dorado had been discovered and consumed.' Of all the places my father wrote about it was Guyana and its tales of gold that held him most in thrall. In his khakis and sturdy boots, machete in hand hacking his way through dense undergrowth, home was wherever he hung his hammock. In *The Marches of El Dorado* he notes that in the Barama Carib language there are no words for happy or unhappy because the Indians find no need for them. It was an outlook he would have envied.

Following in the footsteps of Sir Walter Raleigh, the longings they set out to satisfy may have differed, but for the Doradoistas, 'The man who goes up the Orinoco/Ends up dead, or winds up loco.' Protestant England's reach faltered at the Latin continent; Elizabeth I's Catholic neighbours had beaten her to it. After two failed expeditions to Guyana, Raleigh is remembered for privateering (his Queen's polite word for piracy) and as the first importer of the potato and the tobacco plant.

It's said that Raleigh was the last Englishman to go in search of El Dorado, but with the gold lust of the nineteenth century, Britain's sole colony in South America again promised vast wealth. It was no delusion. There is still gold in Guyana, but its alluvial shifts keep the prospectors at bay, concealing its most precious gift from those whose motive is impure.

Mount Roraima stands at the point where Guyana, Venezuela and Brazil meet. Forbidding and notoriously inaccessible, the table top mountain had haunted my father since he was a boy, when he read Conan Doyle's *The Lost World*. En route through savannah and jungle, he describes a wilderness of 'dark, bamboolike turubans, towering ferns, plants with flapping flag-fronds . . . everything was ice-cold and wet . . . lianas writhed in every direction like endless snakes'. In this perilous and stagnant garden he repeats the word 'Roraima' over and over, as if it's the name of a woman he's in love with. Guarded by swirling clouds and erratic electrical storms, the first successful ascent was in 1885. Since then, few westerners had reached its flat summit of crystal rocks and a thousand waterfalls. Its suspended development promised prehistoric flora: voracious pitcher plants and giant orchids growing in a landscape of volcanic sculptures shaped by the extreme climate. On Roraima there were few signs of life, only ink-black butterflies the size of a man's hand and miniature ebony toads, both unique to the plateau.

When my father made his final footstep, as the rock face suddenly flattened, he wrote: 'During those first astonished moments of arrival it seemed to me that the monsters of the Lost World had been turned into black frigid monoliths.' Moments after the ascent, he made me shout 'hurrah!' for the 1950s English explorer: 'I lunched perched on one of the Druidic rocks; it was a ritual meal brought specially for this day — the best pâté I could find in Georgetown, and a small pot of caviar, each spread on rather damp Norwegian bread ... the ultimate luxury, eating caviar on Roraima.' Then he went one better: he finished his lunch with a slice of Dundee cake.

At the end of his three-week expedition, he returned to base camp, exhausted and elated, his khakis torn and grimy with sweat. As he approached the borrowed bungalow at Kamerang he was surprised to see its light on. He wrote:

Three white men I had never seen before were dining. One, a tall fair young man, rose with a startled look and walked towards me. My hand went out.

'Swan,' I said.

'Attenborough,' said the young man. Each of us metaphorically clicked his heels. It was not until the next morning that we congratulated each other on not saying 'Dr Livingstone I presume.'

He doesn't mention it, but my father and David Attenborough look remarkably alike; perhaps the latter was startled by the sight of his doppelganger at the bungalow door. I wrote to David Attenborough and within the week received the following typed-out notes from his journal, dated 29 April 1955: 'As we sat down to dinner, Michael Swan unexpectedly turned up, having climbed Roraima. Having also not talked to anyone for three weeks, he stopped with us until past midnight.' No doubt eager to share his discoveries, it was probably one of the few occasions when he felt the need to talk instead of listen.

Despite his desire to keep his distance from the reader, my father's delight in the transient is contagious. There are moments when his celebration of life's fleeting rewards remains as vivid as if I were standing beside him in the Guyana jungle at daybreak:

I awoke to sounds that were to prove a misleading augury for our march, a birdsong of a liquid sweetness no magic flute could have emulated, notes that formed music so controlled and logical that it seemed some creating mind had composed it. A theme would be stated, repeated and followed by variations in harmony, sometimes given with all the power the little instrument was capable of, sometimes almost quavering and distant, as if the bird were spent with the passion of its own music. I lay still and listened in my hammock, making no attempt to go to the bush where the bird sang, in case I should frighten it and lose its song. And then, at last, having greeted the morning it ceased its music. I never heard it again.

The Marches of El Dorado

I hear the echo of another augury in his applause for the quadrille bird, a little brown wren of no splendour other than its song. He was captivated by the exotic and brilliantly plumed, 'the trogons and parrots that make the canopy hideous with their shrieks', but his career was in imminent jeopardy from love of the most destructive kind, couched in ostensibly unassuming form.

The little brown wren was Margot Walmsley. My father first met her in 1956 at one of her soirées. Margot was Stephen Spender's managing editor at *Encounter*; along with Cyril Connolly's *Horizon*, it was one of the most important cultural and political journals of its time. Shortly after their first meeting, my father confided in a letter to Maurice Cranston: 'I find myself thinking of Margot constantly. She's one of the kindest and most sweet-natured people you could possibly find.' As they had with many other women, his thoughts strayed easily, but for now his priorities were tidily packaged and he was able to separate the personal from the professional.

She didn't fit his usual criteria. Most of his girlfriends were willowy and blonde; Margot was plump and mousey-haired. She took care over her appearance and dressed elegantly in pastel colours. Her friends remember her long fluttering eyelashes and fluting, theatrical voice with a slight but engaging stammer, and an alluring smile accompanied by a laugh that sounded like bells ringing. Everything about Margot was soft and sweet and warm, like a toasted pink marshmallow. Perry Worsthorne describes her as 'endearing and selfless. She always saw the best side of human nature, almost to a fault.'

Margot was nine years older than my father and widowed with a ten-year-old son. Her friends often talk of her maternal streak and that she loved to take care of other people. As the youngest child of devoted parents, my father grew up with more pampering than was good for him. Margot's little family, and especially her mothering instinct, must have appealed to him: unconditional love with perhaps a hint of rivalry between son and lover — he always needed something to struggle against.

Whether the initial attraction was a sudden bolt of lightning or a slow-burning fuse is hard to tell. Even his confidant Francis King, the recipient of more intimate details than he wanted, knew little about the relationship: 'Michael didn't confide in me about Margot the way he had with other girlfriends. He drew a reverent silence around her, which I took to mean he was in love.' Margot did the same, but for a different reason. 'Everyone knew they were a couple,' Marigold Johnson said, 'but I never really believed it was serious because Margot never talked about him, not once.' My father's discretion was a mark of respect, but it seems Margot's signalled ambivalence.

It's said there are two kinds of people: guests and hosts. My father was most definitely a guest. Margot, on the other hand, was famous for the parties she held at her top-floor flat in Kensington. Funded by *Encounter*, and attended by both grandees and greenhorns, the wine was in generous supply, as well as her preferred tipple — Scotch whisky poured from a crystal decanter. 'Margot was always introducing you to people you'd known for years,' Marigold said. 'She couldn't bear anyone feeling left out or without a full glass in their hand. I remember her dashing from guest to guest asking, 'Darling, have you met so-and-so?' More than once you'd hear the answer, 'Yes, he's my husband.'' Margot was like a mother hen making sure her chicks were comfortable and well watered.

Ambitious as he was, my father valued Margot's position as a literary guardian. She was the gravitational force around which his particular universe revolved: he had found his ideal woman. She was also his mentor and encouraged him to write fiction. There may have been another reason why writing a novel was so crucial at this point: it meant staying in London. Owing to Margot's proximity, home was suddenly an appealing place.

Set in Florence, *The Paradise Garden* is a study in jealousy and betrayal. Frail from teenage rheumatic fever and fussed over by her mother, his heroine is a young English woman — named Anna. She has the love of a reliable and solvent diplomat, but her emotions are ice-capped and she rejects his proposal. On holiday in Florence, following a brief courtship, she marries a dashing but impoverished Anglo-Italian aristocrat named Simon. Simon is half in love with his best friend Marcus, who eventually poisons the marriage. At the close of a torpid Florentine summer, the forsaken Anna races up the steep stairway of a ruined tower near the ancestral castello. Her weakened heart and lungs fail and she dies three days later in hospital, a subtle and slow suicide.

I first read it when I was sixteen, and until then I didn't know I'd been named after the heroine of my father's only novel. It was 1977 and he'd been dead for nearly ten years. With a teenager's ability to dismiss anything that warranted too much consideration, I rarely thought about him, nor did I show off to my friends that my father had been a well-known author. But when I saw my name in his opening sentence I couldn't help but smile. I didn't know what to do with the smile, so I left it where it was. It lasted for the length of the novel.

At that age my critical faculties were non-existent and I couldn't tell whether *The*

Paradise Garden was good, bad or mediocre. I've read it several times in the years since and with each reading its flaws become more apparent. The reviews were politely bland. Cashenden Cass wrote in *Time and Tide*: 'Had the author set his characters in a Kensington square, where they more properly belong, they would be less easy to tolerate. This is a very neat and efficient first novel, with everything — style, plot, dialogue — in its reasonable place.' The *TLS* noted ' . . . a bow or two in the direction of Henry James. *The Paradise Garden* has the virtues of control and careful workmanship; behind it all an acute intelligence is manifestly moving, yet it does leave a doubt whether Mr Swan is really by nature a novelist.' He would have glowed at the reference to James, but winced at what *The Times* had to say: 'Mr Swan has a sympathetic mind and it is all done pleasantly enough although he fails to communicate any sense of urgency or importance.' These last two reviews were unsigned but I suspect the authors were friends of my father's, hinting that he should stick to his day job of travel writing. A more impartial critic might have said: 'Mr Swan ought to take a cold, hard look at his heroine and ask himself where she might have ended up had he allowed her a more resilient disposition.'

A slight novel about a small life, it contains a message my father was deaf to: take a deep breath and face your demons. Her lungs congested and her heart frozen, Anna could do neither. As a travel writer he came across as objective and shrewd, but as a novelist he exposed his neuroses and naivety. Compared to his other books, *The Paradise Garden* reads like a first draft. In his impatience to impress Margot he may have rushed the writing, too eager to hand over the finished manuscript and gain her approval.

He was deeply hurt by the reviews and it was his first and last attempt at fiction. It's also his only book without a dedication. In the copy I have he wrote: 'For dearest Margot, who advised me so bravely and so well. All love, Michael.' I wonder what her advice was and why the book ended up with me and not Margot.

'I could never really see why Margot was such a femme fatale,' the biographer and journalist Anthony Sampson said, 'but she had that effect on a lot of men. Perhaps it's because she was drawn to lame ducks who were living beyond their means and playing roles they couldn't afford or live up to. She was a mother figure to many in that febrile upper bohemian world.' My father must have felt frustrated that he had to share Margot with her expansive circle of friends while aching for her undivided attention.

He turned to her for reassurance in a way he couldn't with his mother. Gwendolyn adored her son but was emotionally withdrawn. Margot was tactile and cuddly and gave him the comfort that had been missing in his childhood. Perhaps for a man intent on the ideal, there is nothing so pure as a mother's love. It might also have been the solution to his conflict between love and lust. Margot gave him everything he needed and asked for little in return. Her life was so full with her other 'children', but for now, second only to her son Alaric, my father was her favourite.

The relationship lasted about eighteen months, his longest by far. Owing to their mutual discretion, I can only guess how they spent their time, but in 1956 romance and turmoil were in the air: Grace Kelly married the prince and Marilyn Monroe the playwright; Soviet tanks encircled Budapest and the Bolshoi Ballet conquered Covent Garden. Margot and my father might well have seen Galina Ulanova's *Giselle*, or strolled hand in hand through Green Park or along the Serpentine, with Alaric flying his kite or chasing pigeons. When my father stayed at Margot's flat in Kensington, there must have been dinners and breakfasts to cook, potatoes to peel and crockery in the sink; the champagne fantasy had finally lost its sparkle in the dishwater of the quotidian.

During this period he wrote three books, *The Paradise Garden*, *British Guiana: The Land of Six Peoples* and *The Marches of El Dorado*, but the inspiration was about to run dry. The end came abruptly, but perhaps not unexpectedly, when Margot fell in love with the playwright Peter Luke. 'Peter was sexy in a brutish sort of way,' Iliana said, 'but he was rather vulgar, in looks as well as bearing, whereas Michael was refined and sensitive, like a poet. He couldn't understand what Margot saw in Peter.' Anthony Sampson agrees, adding, 'Peter was charming and arrogant, and no lame duck.' Margot couldn't help but take care of her friends, but in a lover it seems she needed a manly man who could look after himself. It was God's, or Schiller's, joke that my father didn't fit *her* ideal.

He suffered the humiliation of running into the happy couple at various parties. The thorns of masochism were firmly embedded, but this time there was no consolation in love's familiar torment; rejection and jealousy were a poisonous combination. 'When Margot left him Michael became obsessed,' Francis King says. 'He just couldn't accept that she didn't want him.' He had found and lost the grand passion, and his possessiveness would prove his 'not knowing when to stop'.

Cut adrift in a milieu that was familiar but no longer comforting, his tightly sealed compartments lost their discreteness. Success had come early and perhaps too easily. He was twenty-five when his first book was published and hadn't had to strive too hard to fit the post-post-Bloomsbury mould. As glittering as it seems, my feelings about this cut-glass world are ambivalent. For those of a delicate disposition it was brittle and a touch precious: one sharp jolt and it shattered.

The British stiff upper lip got them through the Blitz but for some it quivered once peace was declared. The insidious protagonist in my father's story was the 1950s itself. Glamorous and grim, emotion-ally repressed yet sexually uninhibited, it was a decade of contradictions, allegedly dwin-dling class consciousness and thwarted idealism. It was also infused with a post-war despondency; with peace came anticlimax. Death was still in the air, and for the unhappy few it beckoned like a treacherous lover.

For my father the decade also brought a lingering sense of guilt and the heightened awareness of his unproven masculinity. He hadn't fought on the Western Front or in Normandy, nor had he lost any close relatives; compared to his contemporaries, he'd had an easy war. He had no valid excuse for his despair and nothing to pin it on, save the collapse of an outworn romantic principle. When the black dog howled in Margot's wake, my father could no longer quieten it; the beast was off the leash and running circles round him.

It was a sign of the times that depression was considered self-indulgent and faintly embarrassing. In the 1950s treatment was limited to sedatives such as tricyclic, but the side-effects were often as bad as the symptoms: drowsiness, anxiety and restlessness. He needed a clear head to write and his only option was the 'get a grip' school of therapy. Surrounded by friends, he had always been an entertaining and playful giggler but I wonder what fears ran through his mind in his own company. He admitted more than once in his first book that he remained *dégagé*, but you can't disengage from your own demons.

For some writers the completion of a manuscript brings elation and relief, for others a dejection that can only be compared to the end of a love affair. For my father it was the latter. He always went home to Emperor's Gate for a few days after delivering a final draft to his publisher. His mother's idea of comfort was a nice pot of Earl Grey and a home-made Victoria sponge, but at least he was in familiar surroundings. 'Granny told me she sometimes heard Michael crying in the night,' my cousin Sheila said, 'but she didn't know how to approach him. In her way, she was as helpless as he was.' During this last visit home, his suffering was twofold.

It was late December 1957. My father was thirty-four and at the height of his success, but Margot had left him within days of his making the final corrections to the proofs of his last book, *The Marches of El Dorado*. He had also recently moved from Shepherd Market to a flat in Roland Gardens, South Kensington. These unconnected events converged, and in the midst of upheaval and despair came a moment of absolute clarity.

Following Somerset Maugham's advice on the spare telling of a story, there are two scenes in this book I can write only as facts. This one was as difficult as the second. My father ought to have been planning his next trip, unpacking his books or shopping for Christmas presents. Instead, he took the Tube from South Ken to Piccadilly Circus. He booked a room in a seedy hotel in Coventry Street, ran a bath and cut his wrists and throat with a razor blade. At around 5 p.m., a hotel chambermaid found him unconscious.

In 1957 attempted suicide was still a crime and a policeman was posted outside his room at Charing Cross Hospital. The loss of blood and oxygen to the brain caused severe neurological damage that left my father with the symptoms of a stroke: paralysis down the right side of his body and aphasia, which erased most of his vocabulary. Meticulous and methodical as he was, he forgot to place the Do Not Disturb sign outside the door. It saved his life but I doubt he would have thanked the poor chambermaid who found him. He never regained his command of language; for a writer it was a slow death.

Francis King recalls the collective shock and guilt: 'None of us realised how desperate he was over Margot. That he chose such a violent method meant it was no mere cry for help.' In severing the two means of communication his downfall was doubly complete. When Francis visited him in hospital he said my father seemed pleased to see him, 'but when he tried to talk, all that emerged was gibberish: 'P-p-please give me that — that p-p-puddle.' I had no idea what

218

he meant. Then I saw he was pointing at a handkerchief that had fallen to the floor beside his bed.' When Francis stood up to leave, he said, 'Michael looked like a child about to be abandoned and he emitted a desolate wail.'

His friends rallied round: Iliana was in Paris when she heard the news and took the first plane back to London; Maurice Cranston organised a visiting rota and Hamish Hamilton, who had published *The Paradise Garden*, set up a trust fund, to which my father's friends contributed for the next ten years. Others did what they could, reading aloud to him or trying to keep him amused with stories of scathing reviews or who got embarrassingly plastered at so-and-so's party. Blank-eyed and bandaged, he lay in his hospital bed and listened without response.

Among his many visitors was Isabel Quigly: 'Margot asked me to go with her to the hospital. I felt terribly uncomfortable and in the way as I was sure he wanted to see her alone.' Isabel remembers the one-sided conversation was awkward and stilted and that nothing much was said. There were no words to ease my father's anguish or Margot's conscience. It was the last time they saw each other.

The only person short on sympathy was his

brother John. 'He seemed more annoyed than anything,' their sister Pauline told me. 'When we left the hospital he said, ''Damn silly thing to do.'' John had been a medical officer in North Africa and France and had helped liberate the concentration camp at Ravensbrück in 1945. Compared to the suffering he'd witnessed, my father's suicide attempt was a selfish and attention-seeking act. Perhaps not untypically of the time, John's compassion had its limits, and his pragmatism prevented him from providing his brother with uncritical support. They were indeed opposites and their paths had diverged long before.

★   ★   ★

In correlation with my father's fixation with ugliness and beauty, certain words recur throughout his books as though they were mutually exclusive. The two most frequent were 'idealism' and 'horror'. He uses 'horror' in place of regret, dissatisfaction and especially disappointment. It's most evident in *The Paradise Garden*, which now reads like a long suicide note. Towards the end of the novel his heroine says: 'The idea of love is something so precious to me that it almost horrifies me . . . yet I want love more than anything else in the world.' My father's standards were so demanding he was unable to accept anything less than the ideal. When it was denied him it left him only one choice: all or nothing.

Margot rose above her own tragedies and never lost her sweetness and generosity. Long before she met my father, her husband had committed suicide, it's said owing to an incurable illness. In 1965, her son, Alaric, gassed himself halfway through his first year at Cambridge. Not surprisingly, her private life was a closed book: she was the person others confided in and it was never reciprocal. She died in 1997, four years before I began my research. Had we met it would have been my most difficult interview by far and I doubt she would have shared her memories of my father with me. If there was any blame attributable it didn't belong with Margot. I wish I'd had the opportunity to say that to her.

'After her son's suicide Margot seemed to shut down,' Perry Worsthorne said. 'There were no other romantic attachments after that and she dedicated herself to her friends.' Sweet as she was, Margot must have felt she was a jinx.

Her obituary in The Times opened with the line: 'Until the very end of her life,

Margot Walmsley was one of London's great party-givers.' She loved to bring people together, and at her flat in Kensington she continued to take new generations of writers under her wing, including Charles Sprawson: 'Margot had extraordinary vitality and empathy and was so easy to talk to. She had such sparkle, and I can see why she was so magical to your father.'

Charles is one of the few people who heard first-hand from Margot any reference to my father: 'When his name came up at one of her parties she still seemed bewildered by what happened. She said she had no idea she'd inspired such passion in him.'

I'd thought the end of their relationship couldn't be any more wretched until Charles told me a story he'd heard from Alan Ross, a close friend of my father's: 'The night before he tried to kill himself, he was standing in the street looking up at Margot's flat and saw her and a man silhouetted in the window. He assumed the man was Peter Luke, but Margot told me he was just a friend she'd invited over for drinks.' This mistaken identity was the trigger for my father's self-destruction.

9

Blind Faith

My mother was twenty-seven and my father thirty-five when they met at Allington Castle, a medieval Carmelite retreat in Kent. He was recuperating from his suicide attempt and she was recovering from her latest romantic disappointment, a brief engagement to an Olympic skier from Finland. My mother had a weakness for broken men and this relationship probably failed because he didn't need healing. My father, however, was as broken as it gets.

Allington Castle is now privately owned but its monastery, Aylesford Priory, is still open to the public. It was my mother's sanctuary, as it was for many writers, Catholic or not. My godmother Dina Barnsley and her family were also frequent visitors. Dina was the dimly remembered figure surrounded by a boisterous brood of children in the big disorderly house with the Bentley in the drive. I knew the Barnsleys had moved to the States some time after I went back to my grandparents. Three years ago I traced Dina to the west coast, where her late husband Alan had been Professor of English at Washington State University. We met again after more than thirty-five years when she came to England to visit family.

It was a sunny day in June when Dina showed me around the priory grounds. It's a beautiful setting with rose gardens and immaculate lawns and a stark 1960s chapel incongruously placed within thirteenth-century walls. Mid-way through our tour we sat on a bench overlooking the white-washed courtyard. Dina told me my mother was very depressed when she first met her at Allington Castle in 1958: 'She'd lost her way and was looking for someone or something to hold on to. I'm sure you know she was considering taking vows.' I'd heard this from various sources, including Grandma. As a child I couldn't understand why anyone would want to be a nun locked up in a convent, but now it sounded like a last-hope solution to an unhappy love life. Dina said she was very devout and quite serious about it until she met my father.

'Your mother had a romantic outlook on life. Her role model was the countess Alessandra di Rudini, Garibaldi's lover, and Joan had it in her mind that she would be a consort to a great man.' I knew she'd added

Alexandra as her middle name by deed poll. Its inspiration fitted with her teenage daydreams of castles and a valiant knight on a white horse; she'd even held the title countess, fake though it was. There were, however, inaccuracies in the timeline and finer points. Alessandra was a marchioness and the mistress of the poet and dramatist Gabriele D'Annunzio, a World War I hero who was created a prince in 1924. When the affair ended some years earlier, Alessandra retreated into a life of prayer, and with family money, restored the Carmelite monastery at Haute-Savoie in the French Alps. She died in 1931, the year my mother was born.

Dina went on to call her 'your very brilliant mother' but said she was uncertain of her own talent: 'When she met your father she believed she would leave her mark as the wife of a celebrated author.' She'd found her fairytale ending, but her knight was lame, mute and half blind.

My father was also inhabiting a fantasy of his own making. *The Paradise Garden* was published in 1956, but in the figure of Anna it was as if he'd already created my mother on the page: her health delicate from teenage rheumatic fever (related to Sydenham's chorea), fickle and impulsive, she fell for a titled philanderer in Florence and eventually died for hopeless love. Recovering at Allington Castle, his mind addled, my father might have thought he'd met his heroine.

As much as I liked Dina, a nagging doubt sat between us on that courtyard bench, accompanied by my unhappy childhood memories. The air was still and oppressive with the scent of incense and roses. It was a pleasant and peaceful backdrop but I didn't feel any sense of spirituality. I didn't see any monks, or gardeners, or any other visitors; in fact there was little sign of life at all. The priory felt as spooky as a struck film set.

Our day together was unsettling for many reasons but Dina's account of my early childhood and her family's part in it reinforced my doubts. I was sure I hadn't seen the Barnsleys since I was about four, but Dina insisted I was seven: 'When we moved to America, Alan felt we shouldn't take you away from your family. That was the only reason we gave you back to your grandparents.' I asked if she was certain of the dates. 'Oh yes,' she said, 'you were with us for five years.' Her version didn't fit with what I remembered but at that point I had no evidence to disprove it.

When I kissed Dina goodbye, it was with some relief. I'd spent my early years longing to get away from the Barnsleys, and that day at Aylesford Priory was no different. She's a nice woman but I couldn't help associating the incense and roses with a fragrant smokescreen.

Not long after I saw Dina, among various family papers such as birth and marriage certificates, my Uncle Howard found a two-page document from the High Court of Justice. On 10 October 1962, a month after my mother died, my father filed for custody, citing the Barnsleys as my potential guardians. My grandparents were named as defendants.

During the hearing, my father's counsel obtained affidavits from Grandma's doctors stating that she was addicted to various prescription drugs, undergoing electroconvulsive therapy following a nervous breakdown brought on by my mother's death and that she was unfit to take care of an infant. My godfather Alan Barnsley, on the other hand, was an upstanding member of the community, a doctor and a successful novelist, under the pen name Gabriel Fielding. The Barnsleys were upper-middle class and intellectual, whereas my grandparents were barely educated and little more than domestics.

In March 1963 my father won the case and I was sent to live with the Barnsleys. The judge had taken them at face value but recently I found a different perspective from two friends who knew the family well. By this stage I was sick and tired of white lies and distorted facts. While I have no wish to offend the surviving Barnsleys, I'm telling it like it is.

'No doubt Dina painted a rosy picture but it was a terribly disorganised and unstable household, and none too clean,' the first friend said. 'Alan was prone to depression and very demanding with Dina's time, so the children were rarely disciplined and didn't get much attention.' Now I know why I had trouble conjuring up the grown-ups, though I recall the anarchy well: it was like a lawless playground with no monitors in sight. When they found my hiding place behind the sofa, the older children played with me as if I were a new toy in the shape of a shatterproof doll; I think they wanted to see how far they could go before the doll broke. I remember one of them pushing me into the tumble drier and switching it on. It was probably only for a few seconds and at the time I no doubt thought it was as funny as they did, but left unsupervised, their games came perilously close to dangerous.

'Alan soon regretted taking you in,' she went on. 'You were such an adorable little thing and visitors always made a big fuss of you at the expense of his own children.' Alan had his good points: he was charming and charitable but fickle and crafty with it. There was a slightly manic energy to his playful teasing. I didn't like it when he picked me up and swung me round in circles; he smelled like an ashtray for one thing, but I always felt he was about to let go of my arms with a mad cackle.

The Barnsleys were devout Catholic converts and Alan liked to be seen to be doing good works: 'He was as determined as your father to win the custody case against your grandparents,' she said, 'but once he'd achieved a goal he often lost interest. They did a terrible thing in taking you away from your mother's family. Anyone could see you belonged with your grandparents.'

'Initially, Alan was very sympathetic to Michael's situation,' the second friend told me. 'He assured him you were both part of the family, but shambolic as the Barnsleys were, there were never any regulations laid down, and when they were it was too late. Michael was difficult at the best of times, gruff and surly because he couldn't communicate properly, but he became too frequent and disruptive a visitor. Eventually, Alan was thoroughly fed up with his demands to see you. I think it was Christmas 1964 that Alan told Michael he could come for lunch but he couldn't stay at the house. Of course there was no transport, so he was stuck in London. I asked Michael where he'd gone for Christmas lunch, and he said, 'The Ritz, where else?' It was a dignified but terribly sad gesture.'

Dina's picture was indeed rosy; Alan's banishment of my father was the nasty trick up the magician's sleeve I'd spotted as a child. 'After that Alan's sympathy finally ran out,' she went on, 'and in a fit of pique he sent you back to your grandparents.' My father was out in the cold: exiled by Alan and a pariah at Grandma's.

Both friends estimated that I lived with the Barnsleys for two years or so, which tallies with the High Court document: March 1963 to November 1965, though I would have gone back to my grandparents at least a couple of months before the final court hearing. In time for the start of the academic year, the Barnsleys probably moved to Washington State in the summer of 1966. 'Dina's discrepancy isn't hard to justify,' the first friend said. 'No doubt she misremembered the past because she didn't want to hurt your feelings, but more importantly to protect her husband's memory.'

Alan Barnsley seemed an incongruous figure among my father's other friends. 'I didn't take to him at all,' Francis King said. 'He struck me as self-important and pompous, with a rather high opinion of his own novels.' I tried to read Alan's best-known book, *The Birthday King*. A line from the opening paragraph indicates why I couldn't get past the first few pages: 'the crepuscular buzz of the universe seeping down through the ionised layer whose depths it was the observatory's purpose to measure.' To be fair, the baroque style might have been a backlash against the austerity of the previous decade when rationing and shortages permeated culture as well as the daily grind.

When *The Birthday King* was nominated for the W.H. Smith Prize for Literature in 1963, Dina told me my father tore up his invitation to the ceremony. She put it down to jealousy but I believe there was more to it than that. My father could no longer read or write, but he would have remembered Alan's earlier books. His own writing was at times florid and adjective-heavy but compared to Alan's it's almost plain English. I think my father tore up the invitation because Alan's work offended his literary sensibilities: even the jacket blurb for *The Birthday King* concedes its author 'has tended to remain an acquired taste'. My father must have been outraged when it won the prize.

Between Dina's scatty goodwill and Alan's crafty games, from 1958 to 1965 the Barnsleys helped and hindered my family. Back at Allington Castle, in 1958, another force was at work, in his way as wily as the chain-smoking magician. My parents' first meeting was set up by my father's friend Archie Colquhoun. A man of many talents and continually in pursuit of a cause, he was an artist, heroic figure to the partisans, Anglo-Italian cultural liaison and translator of Manzoni's *The Betrothed* and Lampedusa's *The Leopard*. An expert in Italian literature, Archie would have known all about Alessandra di Rudini's calling and may well have persuaded my mother to follow a similar mission in restoring my father.

Archie was also a heavy drinker, notorious troublemaker and a recently unlapsed Catholic. Not long before his match-making at the castle, he'd been an ardent Communist, until he saw a vision of the Virgin Mary on a beach in Majorca. Mary spoke to him at length, no doubt berating him for his atheism among other things. He claimed this vision changed his life and propelled a swift return to the Church.

Archie saw himself as a fixer, but capricious and cracked as he was, misfortune seeped out of him and it was usually at someone else's expense. There could hardly have been a more inauspicious figure to act as a go-between for my parents: later implicated in the death of the historian Richard Rumbold, Archie couldn't help interfering in his friends' lives. While an undergraduate at Oxford, Richard had been excommunicated by the university's chaplain, under orders from the Bishop of Birmingham, after publishing a scandalous novel, *Little Victims*, based on his adolescent sexual experiences at Eton. He was a wealthy, blond Adonis with a taste for anonymous sex, as well as a profound guilt complex fuelled by his Catholic upbringing. Along with a trust fund it seems he also inherited a fateful birthright: his mother and sister had committed suicide.

In March 1961 Richard and Archie were touring Sicily together when Archie encouraged him to take communion, having forgotten he'd already told the priest that his friend and the Church had long parted company. In front of a massed congregation in Palermo, Richard was refused communion. The following day he jumped from the bathroom window of their hotel. Whether Archie's sins were venial or mortal is debatable, but when he died of cirrhosis three years later he must have had a hard time talking his way past St Peter.

Archie saw in my parents a delicate woman with a tentative vocation and a damaged man in need of a saviour, and leaped to the wrong conclusion. Now a fervent papist, Archie's blind faith prevented him from seeing this union for what it was: the light at the end of the tunnel was the light of an oncoming train, as Robert Lowell once wrote. Quoted in the *Daily Express* in a news item about my father's impending marriage, Archie said: 'I suppose you could call Michael's recovery a miracle of love. Miracles happen all the time.' In fact, my father hadn't recovered. He was still partially paralysed and monosyllabic. When over-tired or fractious, he communicated by scrawling a few words on a small slate with a piece of chalk in his left hand; his ambidextrous party trick was now a necessity.

My mother's depression on her arrival at Allington Castle lifted as soon as she set eyes on my father. She'd found her celebrated author. He was a bit battered and brooding but she could easily heal him. As soon as he was back on his feet she would help him with research, type up his manuscripts and proof-read galleys. There would be lunches at the Reform and cocktails at the Gargoyle, and parties hosted by the Spenders and the Connollys, proudly standing at her husband's side. As for my father, he must have been relieved that Archie had presented him with such an agreeable and selfless nurse. She wasn't really his type, but she was attractive enough and seemed docile and willing.

My parents recognised in each other more than the urgent fulfilment of her fairytale and his remedial needs: theirs was a narcissistic meeting of minds. It was no 'miracle of love', nor a moonstruck movie moment accompanied by the soaring strings of an invisible orchestra.

Archie was a fast worker and very pleased with himself for saving these two lost souls. My parents were married within the month, on 20 November 1958 at St Francis Church in Maidstone. An article in the *Kent Messenger* begins: 'Michael Swan, the 35-year-old author who has been living in a castle owned by the Carmelites, has married in secret.' Archie may have exaggerated the secrecy, since my mother goes on to say, 'We wanted to keep it quiet and avoid any fuss, though naturally our relatives knew we were getting married.' Either the family wasn't invited or Grandma had once again voiced her disapproval — penniless, posh and a cripple: I doubt she could have imagined a more unpromising son-in-law. The article's déjà vu headline, 'Bride in a Castle', was an omen my mother either missed or chose to ignore.

She wore a dove-grey Audrey Hepburn frock and white gloves. Archie made sure the groom looked smart in a suit and tie, before he ushered him up the aisle in a wheelchair. The priest must have made a concession over the vows since my father couldn't manage much more than 'I do.' Owing to their brief courtship and my mother's hasty nature, she paid no attention to the words 'in sickness and in health'.

Shortly after the wedding my parents moved to Majorca, where my father's friend Hugh Gibb loaned them his villa rent-free. It had no electricity or gas, its sole amenity was a cold-water tap. In 1929 Gertrude Stein said of the island: 'It's paradise, if you can stand it.' Thirty years later it remained unspoiled by tourism. A bolt-hole for artists, beatniks and a few incipient hippies, over the previous decades writers such as Arthur Rackham, D.H. Lawrence and Anaïs Nin had passed through. Kingsley Amis and his family were intermittent visitors, as were Hollywood stars including Ava Gardner. Its most famous permanent resident was Robert Graves, who my father first met at Faber during the war. When my parents went to dinner at the Graves' in nearby Deià, my father spent the evening in a scowling, hostile sulk, as he frequently did in the company of writers he'd known as an up-and-coming young man of letters: the author of *I, Claudius* and one of Britain's greatest love poets reminded my father of his lost career. My mother probably did her best to excuse his boorish behaviour but they weren't invited again.

With such august neighbours and in tranquil surroundings, she should have thrived on the island but her days were occupied with looking after her disabled, anti-social husband. Cooking was always a challenge, or guess-work, for my mother, especially on two rings of a Primus stove. She was used to over-poached kippers, lumpy mash and limp cabbage, but here they ate fish from the local market and green olives and red capsicum. In England food slopped, in Spain it was so fresh it almost danced on your plate, to the accompaniment of sangria floating with fruit. It was an insular existence, though there were devotional compensations: the villa overlooked the beach where Archie had met the Virgin Mary. With her bare feet on Catholic sand, my mother may well have found spiritual company.

Her writing career put to one side to kick-start her husband's, she was determined to see his name in print again. She spent much of her time supervising his physio-therapy, reading aloud to him and teaching him to speak using exercises from a speech therapy manual. She also reworked his poems, a few of which ran in the *Listener* and the *London Magazine*. Despite the scrambled syntax his former colleagues gave him the benefit of the doubt.

I'm taking an unqualified shot in the dark here, but his poem entitled 'Palinurus' indicates a mind grasping for a metaphorical message. The final stanza reads:

Roaring and tempest, unpeaceful sea,
Failing heart breaks and dies.
Deserted coast and sand, a boatman
    cries —
'Palinurus is dying! I see his ghost.'

Palinurus was the sacrificial helmsman in Virgil's *Aeneid*, a shadow in the Underworld awaiting passage across the Styx. It was also the pseudonym Cyril Connolly used for *The Unquiet Grave* (1944), which explored 'the core of melancholy and guilt that works destruction on us from within.' The poem was published in *Encounter* — the rival to Connolly's *Horizon* — and reads like a coded reproach to Margot.

In a letter from Majorca to John Lehmann,

my mother wrote that the enclosed 'poems have been written by an 'aphasic' i.e. a person suffering from a complete breakdown of the know-how of expression either in speech or writing. It's Michael's first attempt at getting back to writing and a great incentive for him. I hope at the end of this year he will be writing fully once more.' It was a vain hope and something of a ruse.

I wonder how long it was before my mother realised she was fighting a lost cause. Along with his speech and mobility, my father had destroyed his personality. The sensitive, even-tempered charmer was gone, his appealing qualities replaced with frustration and irritability, on a good day. At his worst he was like an aggressive child caught in a tantrum and powerless to communicate. Vocal dexterity had not only been a means of support but of entertainment and seduction; now he was verbally impotent. Isolated on Majorca as they were, my mother took the flack, with increasingly fading hope of the literary partnership she'd imagined.

About six weeks before I was born, in December 1960, my parents returned to London. During my first few months we lived in the flat in Roland Gardens, South Kensington, which my father's friends had sublet while he recovered from his suicide attempt. 'By this time your mother was terribly strained and tense, and trapped in a shell of a marriage,' Dina said. 'One day she told me she was crossing Westminster Bridge with you and saw the handle of your pram as her only anchor on life.'

My mother used to put whisky in my milk to send me to sleep. Pre-Calpol, it was a common practice and known as mummy's secret sedative; she must have needed a rest from both my and my father's need of her care and attention. I hadn't realised until now that most of my baby pictures are of my mother and me. I have no photographs of the three of us, and none of my father and me together. It's as if my mother didn't have the energy to lift the camera, or perhaps she already knew we were a family destined for separation.

We went back to Majorca for about six months, until the money from Hamish Hamilton's trust fund and an annual grant of £100 from the Royal Literary Fund could no longer support us. Shortly before we returned to Roland Gardens, in a letter to Maurice and Iliana Cranston dated 18 March 1961, my mother said: 'I am very sorry to have to write like this but I desperately need a loan of £200. I realise the enormous amount, but I have the rent to pay, rates and I am in arrears with the electricity and telephone bills. Is it at all possible that on the basis of repaying you at £3 a week, that you could possibly help us out? PS I'm being sued for the rates.' I couldn't help note the 'I' in her letter. The responsibility for our family lay squarely on her slight shoulders and she was reduced to begging for money from friends. Iliana and Maurice gave us the loan, which I doubt was ever repaid.

At this time Alan Barnsley's benefaction towards my parents was at its peak. He and Dina arranged a mortgage on a cottage in the village of Chart Sutton, not far from their house in Maidstone. Dina telephoned their friend Graham Greene, explaining my father's circumstances. Quietly charitable to promising young writers in financial straits, he immediately wrote a cheque for the down payment on the cottage. He even offered to take my father on to his staff at £300 a year, but Dina had to tell him how incapacitated he was. I find it difficult to reconcile the Barnsleys' generosity with Alan's later behaviour, but for now he was firmly on my parents' side. It was around this time that my mother's literary ruse manifested itself.

What little strength she had was waning, and she left my father on several occasions, taking me with her to her parents in London. Each time she was lured back by his need of her caretaking and ghost-writing skills. During their three-year marriage she wrote the introduction to a Penguin collection of Henry James's short stories, a few book reviews and a column in the *Listener*, the BBC's weekly journal — all under my father's name. As Leigh Adams, my mother was almost unknown but the by-line Michael Swan guaranteed commission.

Aside from the financial necessity, this masquerade was an extension of her need to shelter behind a name other than her own; in print she was always one step removed. My guess is she was comfortable with the pretence, but it must have been humiliating for my father. He'd always been more interested in hearing other people's stories than relating his own, and now he had a column his wife wrote for him in a journal whose masthead embodied one of his most prized attributes.

By the late 1950s audience ratings for television had over-taken radio's, and the *Listener*'s circulation dropped from 133,600 in 1955 to around 100,000 in 1961. In 'The Spoken Word', my mother reviewed items broadcast on the Home Service and more often the Third Programme, a network denounced in certain quarters for its élitism. As well as the arts, she covered a wide variety of subjects including fox-hunting, censorship, the Mafia, alcoholism and birth control. Influenced by her Catholicism and her time working for Karl Popper, she was drawn to religious and philosophical debate, whether discussing the censor in society or Sicily's perverted chivalry. Writing as Michael Swan allowed her to stand more firmly behind her arguments, but she soon set herself up for criticism:

> Love of wisdom erects no barriers. Dr A.L. Rowse, the historian, is a perfect example of what a man can achieve despite his background. Dr Rowse talked with the poet Charles Causley of his upbringing in a working-class home in Cornwall, with uneducated parents, but much affection. Once again we were told of the loneliness of the intellectual life, of solitude with occasional friendship. The choice seems predetermined, and it seems that those who can escape the working-class environment do so very quickly.

The words loneliness, solitude and escape resound like a minor triad, as though she's writing of her own background as much as Causley's.

She begins her column of 8 February 1962: 'I have never plumbed the depths which separate literary criticism from radio criticism — perhaps that is why I am accused, anonymously of course, of being too 'personal' in this column. I wonder what other critics do with such letters? Do they keep them, provided they're flattering, or do they ignore them?' Rather than defend her approach, she recommends literary v. radio criticism as a potential subject for *Woman's Hour*, which was a bit of a giveaway considering 'The Spoken Word' was supposed to be written by a man.

Her style is indeed personal, but in drifting from the programmes under discussion she brings insight and a light touch to serious topics. Writing of a series on lost memories, she recalls an anecdote about the essayist and critic Edmund Gosse's first meeting with James Joyce:

'Young man, there isn't enough chaos in your mind.' There may not have been chaos as Gosse understood it, but there was certainly contained in James Joyce's brain a world of unsuspected imagination and humour. In a café in Geneva,

Joyce kept asking the waitress for lemon-squash and she kept replying 'Yes, quite true'. This went on until he insisted that what he really wanted was a lemon-squash. 'Oh, I'm sorry,' she replied, 'I thought you said *Lebens quatsch*!' (life's nonsense). It was this nonsensicality of daily life that Joyce gave us in his later work.

If only she could have brought this light-heartedness home, but I don't imagine our little cottage often rang with the sound of laughter. Along with his cheekiness and delightful giggle, my father had lost all trace of humour, while my mother didn't have much to smile about.

Reviewing a programme entitled *Love Letters*, she wrote:

We were given a glimpse of the personality behind the pen — the private individual committing to paper words from the heart, intended only for the recipient, not for the public. There is usually a spontaneity in the letter-form which releases any inhibitions and one feels free to confess on paper what one would normally conceal in speech. There is no fear of saying the wrong thing — a certain boldness creeps in and the writer finds himself unable to stop the flow of words.

Both my parents wrote such letters, but not to each other. Despite my mother's views on postal privacy, her very last love letter would end up in the public domain, three times over. Had she known her daughter would one day read so personal a correspondence her spontaneity might well have wavered.

Rather than assume my father's style, she adapted it and cut back on the erudition. The *Listener*'s editor, Maurice Ashley, believed the column was my father's work, but he must have been puzzled that his voice had changed so dramatically. The tone was softer and the timbre ingenuous, as if my mother were calling to the reader, 'Come and sit next to me, I have something to tell you.' Compared to my father, she preferred to remain *engagé*.

She wrote these columns at the mahogany desk that now stands in an alcove in my living room. When I press my hand against its surface I can almost feel her presence absorbed in the grain of the wood. Its veneer is scored in places, some of the scars hers and some mine, but I can no longer tell the difference. In my late teens I sat at this desk as I practised typing on her clunky manual Smith Corona. It was eggshell blue with grey keys and its ribbon frayed and faint, unchanged since she last used it. As I tapped out 'qwerty' I was aware of her fingertips there before mine. When I read the published results of my mother's old typewriter I felt her looking over my shoulder, willing me to read between the lines. Her words told me she was vibrant, witty and unafraid to speak her mind. But this spirited woman seemed to exist only on the page.

10

Forbidden Love

As a teenager, phenobarbitone had left my mother's reception fuzzy, but her dependency on prescription drugs was now an addiction, and included amphetamines to counteract the morning-after fatigue of barbiturates. She didn't have the time or inclination to cook proper meals; fast food came in tins and packets labelled Heinz and Bird's Eye. The pressures on her as breadwinner, nursemaid to an invalid and mother to an infant left her worn out and running on empty.

Apparently I was a good-as-gold baby; I slept and gurgled happily to myself. I was no trouble, whereas my father was truculent and demanding. Disillusion must have set in on Majorca, but after three years of so-called marriage and her valiant but vain attempts to rehabilitate my father, she'd finally had enough. She left him for good in March 1962. Shortly after deserting her post as keeper of the literary flame, she called the *Listener*'s editor and owned up to the subterfuge. Mr Ashley was none too pleased he'd been hoodwinked but, stuck for a contributor, he allowed her to write two columns under her pseudonym Leigh Adams.

Released from her husband's by-line, her last column was dated 12 April 1962. Reviewing a programme on Tchaikovsky, she cites the Violin Concerto as her favourite piece of music. It's also mine. Long before I discovered our shared love for it, I'd always sensed a significance beyond its emotional intensity. At home or in the concert hall, it left me longing for something I couldn't quite place. Listening to it as I write this paragraph, I recognise the solo violin's yearning for the impossible.

My mother and I moved in with my grandparents at Hyde Park Gardens. Grandma was delighted to have her daughter back at home. She needed feeding up and pampering after everything that no-good husband of hers had put her through: Grandma had been right all along, he was a bad lot. It's anyone's guess how Grandpa felt.

During my parents' first year on Majorca, my mother had somehow found time to write my father's biography. Now that she was back in London she made the most of his connections. Raleigh Trevelyan was then a director at Michael Joseph: 'We met at my office and she brought in a rather bulky manuscript based on your father's life, but we couldn't publish it because it was potentially libellous, especially with regard to his brother John.'

My father and John hadn't fallen out as such until the suicide attempt, when he'd tried to gain power of attorney and have my father committed. John had married an heiress and consequently had appearances to keep up; it seems my father was an embarrassment to his respectable GP brother. Years earlier he'd nicknamed John's big house in Ealing, Eel Pie Palace. At that time my father thought him a social climber and a snob, but from 1958 the two of them were engaged in internecine warfare, erasing all memory of their fighting the enemy side by side as boys at Emperor's Gate. Remembering John's kindness and generosity to me in his later years, it's hard to square these discrete aspects. They were indeed two peas in a fraternal pod, each with his own multi-faceted personality.

When Raleigh told me about the libellous manuscript it set me on a three-year search. Not only would it hold the answers to many questions, I wanted to know how my mother followed the trajectory of the story and how much of herself she placed in it, struggling as I was to find my place in this story. It was a huge disappointment but no great surprise to learn it had been thrown out with the rubbish in 1968.

Among the proofs and press releases on Raleigh's desk was a photograph of one of his writers. 'I remember Joan staring at it. I didn't realise at the time but it was a pivotal moment in her life. It was probably me who introduced them, much to my regret.' The black and white portrait was of the author and critic Kay Dick.

In May 1962 my mother wrote to her sister-in-law, Marsli: 'I went out last night with a woman writer, Kay Dick, but was sick most of the evening . . . a lovely old house in Flask Walk, Hampstead, and tons of gossip.' Among the other guests were the novelists Olivia Manning and Isobel English and her husband Neville Braybrooke. Literary London was as close-knit as it had been five years earlier when my father belonged to the West End faction. Membership was by invitation or association and my mother used her husband's name as a calling card. Despite his self-imposed isolation, his friends, including Raleigh and Kay, welcomed her as an affiliate. As a key member, Kay was ardent in her professional and social relationships but drew little distinction between the two. With her sharp intelligence and biting with she charmed nearly everyone who met her, until the squabbles and feuds she instigated brought so many friendships to a bitter end.

'For Kay, life was a melodrama,' Francis King said, 'and she was always the protagonist.' She wore a monocle as much for effect as poor eyesight and often dressed for dinner in a tuxedo and bow-tie. With her short blonde hair, pronounced features and an ever-present cigarette in a mother-of-pearl holder, she looked like Alec Guinness in the guise of a lesbian littérateur. 'She was the last graduate of Radclyffe Hall,' her former friend Peter Burton observed, referring to the authoress whose novel *The Well of Loneliness* was banned in the 1920s for obscenity, 'yet Kay adamantly denied she was a lesbian. I think she saw herself as a straight man.' Averse to labels of any kind, she was a one-off.

In the black and white photograph that so transfixed my mother, Kay looks like the wicked witch of north-west London casting her spell with a cigarette holder in place of a wand. After my mother's meeting with Raleigh she wrote Kay a fan letter in praise of her article on Colette in the *Saturday Book*. My mother had recently translated and adapted Colette's 1944 novella *The Cat*, which was broadcast on the Home Service shortly before she met Kay; Colette was the subject of one of Kay's books that would never be finished; my mother's first piece for the *Listener* ran beside a review of Kay's book *Pierrot*, which Raleigh had commissioned. Fodder for a fertile imagination, these coincidences would no doubt have struck my mother as romantic destiny.

An avid admirer of Colette's work as well as her bisexual lifestyle, she might have come across the following quotes: 'You will do foolish things, but do them with enthusiasm'; and 'I believe there are more urgent and honourable occupations than the incomparable waste of time we call suffering.' Inhabiting the first, she missed the message in the second. For my mother, suffering came as naturally as breathing.

Kay and I met thirteen years ago, at her basement flat on the seafront at Brighton; she'd left Hampstead in 1968 in pursuit of an ex-lover. Francis told me that she was a close friend of my mother's just before she died. He also warned, 'She can be quite fierce if you catch her in the wrong mood.' At that time I knew so little about my mother and Kay was the first of her few friends I would meet.

On the train from Victoria I was intrigued but a little nervous, hoping to catch her in fair weather. At a bookshop near the clock tower I found several of her titles in the local authors section. On the inside jacket of one was a photograph taken in her late thirties. Elegantly dressed and coiffed, and haloed in a cloud of cigarette smoke, she looked . . . suave. I bought the book next to it because I liked the cover, a Picasso-style collage of two women. It was called *The Shelf*.

Kay was waiting for me at the top of the steps to her flat. She didn't return my smile as we shook hands and her mood was hard to read. At seventy-six she was slightly stooped and her hair white and uncombed. Her vanity long gone, she was dressed in what appeared to be her gardening clothes, baggy beige trousers and what was once a cashmere V-neck jumper. It was a bright afternoon in mid July, but the front room was dimly lit and the curtains drawn. The bookshelves were full to overflowing and much of the carpet was piled high with newspapers and magazines. The walls and ceiling were tanned with nicotine and the air smelled of powdery paper, the dusty scent of decay usually found only in archives. On a table by the window sat an old electric typewriter.

Kay served tea in delicate china cups and smoked her way through a plate of cucumber sandwiches with the crusts cut off. She had a weakness for cream meringues and I couldn't keep pace, with the cakes or the fags. As we talked I was aware of her studying me through eyes blanched with cataracts, but her manner was milder and more sympathetic than I'd expected.

Her voice softened when she spoke of my mother but her observations were vague and non-committal: 'Joan was a difficult person to get to know. She was unsure of herself and complicated.' I said that trying to capture my mother was like grasping at air. 'Or quicksilver,' she said. 'Joan wasn't someone who gave much away. Just like your father.'

Looking now at my notes from our meeting, my questions must have been routine and naïve since Kay's answers were frustratingly oblique: 'I don't think she was ever really happy, and certainly not during her marriage.' That came as no surprise, but I was puzzled when she said, out of the blue: 'Has no one in your family ever mentioned me?' They hadn't. I asked what she meant but she dismissed it with a wave of her hand. Knowing that she liked to be the centre of attention, I misinterpreted the gesture and thought she was offended at the lack of acknowledgement, but I hit a nerve when I said I'd always sensed a disapproval of my parents' friends: 'I never met Joan's parents, nor did I want to, but she was desperate to get away from home. She was suffocating in that over-protective atmosphere.' It was obviously a touchy topic so I let it pass for the moment.

The mood lightened and the conversation drifted pleasantly enough, but when I brought it back to my mother Kay became irritable: 'I only knew her for a few months, and I really don't think I have anything more to tell you.' The subject was apparently closed.

At that time I was trying to write my parents' story as a novel and Kay was keen to help with research. She put me in touch with several contacts, including her agent, and even offered to read the finished manuscript. In retrospect, there may have been an ulterior motive in her offer. Towards the end of our meeting she said, almost coyly, 'You might discover things you don't want to know.' When I told her I wanted to know everything, she raised her eyebrows and said: 'Be careful what you wish for.' I ought to have asked why she was being so cagey but I had the feeling I would find out from another source what she was concealing.

As I said goodbye at the door she peered at me through the magnifying glass she wore around her neck and smiled for the first time. 'Yes, you look so like her,' she said. My hair was long then, almost to my waist, while my mother wore hers in an Elizabeth Taylor style. I was near enough the same age as my mother during their brief friendship, but I had a suspicion Kay and I wouldn't step beyond acquaintance, and that I would have to tread carefully. She was prickly and unpredictable, but I rather liked her fierce energy, and her appetite for cakes.

On the train home I began reading *The Shelf*. Published in 1984, it's an autobiographical novel related in the form of a letter to Francis King. Its opening line sounded like a defence for a misjudged and unsolicited affair. Halfway down the second page I realised why Kay had been so furtive. Anne, as Kay names the erstwhile lover, died some twenty years earlier, followed shortly after by her husband Maurice. After meeting their now grown-up daughter, the narrator refers to her as the orphan, and goes on to describe her auburn hair and resemblance to her mother. Kay hadn't seen me since I was a baby but it was obvious that 'Anne' was my mother. I ought to have been shocked by this revelation but I wasn't. It fitted perfectly in a jigsaw made up of whispered secrets and misinformation.

I finished reading *The Shelf* late that night, my mind reeling with a thousand different thoughts, but the most immediate was: 'Bloody hell! My mother inspired a novel!' Kay's portrayal was a mass of contradictions: calculating and innocent, deceitful and transparent, she was both vixen and victim. Kay wasn't exaggerating when she said she was difficult to get to know. The plot, however, was authentic. It would take more than a decade, but when I eventually uncovered the truth about my mother's death I found that Kay's account was as precise as it was misleading.

The next day I sent her a thank you note and tactfully asked how much of *The Shelf* was based on fact. She wrote back with a veiled disclosure, admitting only that it was a novella. With her letter she enclosed a book token for £10, a gesture I knew she couldn't afford. Habitually broke but prone to random acts of generosity, she often bought gifts for her friends and herself. 'Kay was a beggar and always borrowing money,' Raleigh told me, 'which she spent on taxis, tailored suits and trinkets for her current flame. The loans were never repaid.' Kay was profligate and proud of it; she lived for the moment and believed money should be squandered not saved.

Authentic as the plot is, rereading *The Shelf* I have to keep reminding myself that it's a roman à clef published over twenty years after the event, and skewed through the lens of Kay's monocle. Only Francis and Raleigh knew about the affair at the time and are best placed to separate artifice from reality. When I asked Francis how true to life *The Shelf* was, he said, 'Kay wasn't someone who could invent things easily,' something of a drawback for a novelist but a valuable resource for me. 'It was a ready-made story,' Raleigh said, 'and Kay exploited it to the full.'

As my mother had written in her letter to Marsli, in *The Shelf* she's ill with flu when she first meets Kay at one of her dinner parties in Hampstead. Within days of meeting, Kay has my mother chasing her with love notes and late night phone calls in a one-sided pursuit. The novel hinges on this correspondence and some of my mother's dialogue is appropriated from her letters, including a chameleon admission that she felt unable to be herself and allowed her image to conform to more than one man's fantasy.

Kay claims my mother was compliant when it suited her, but well aware of her sensuality and its effect on men. Her courtesan's eyes always on the lookout, she used her femininity as a defensive weapon, as Kay observes with almost too much admiration; when provoked my mother's Mediterranean blue eyes flashed ice cold.

The Shelf is the gospel according to Kay. Apocryphal as it is, I've tried to see past the bias in search of my mother's true character. My copy is yellowed with Post-it Notes, dog-eared and almost every page marked in pencil, but I still can't find her. Perhaps it's because the protagonists in my parents' story so often concealed themselves behind the printed page: my father masked and detached from the reader, my mother publishing her work under his name, and Kay's unacknowledged pilfering from my mother's letters.

About halfway through the novel, she has the grace to question her facsimile, and wonders whether she might have crafted an untruthful likeness for her own amusement. Yes and no would be my answer, though one or two observations hit home. Kay's analysis is astute: my mother appeared friendless and unable to settle in one place; her severance from personal resourcefulness was a reflection of her rarefied nature; she was a hothouse flower in need of tender nurturing. Later, my mother says: 'All my life I've searched for love but never found it.' What little Kay offered didn't include love, but it seems my mother believed her search was over.

This sexual awakening relieved some of her anxieties, but it also provoked new ones, the need for secrecy and deception among them, traits that apparently came easily. Mystique, however, was part of her allure, though Kay writes that she was frequently irritated and even enraged with my mother for her duplicity and evident disloyalty.

For Kay the attraction was predominantly physical. Thankfully she stops short of lascivious description, but the intensity my mother inspired suggests that sex was the one arena in which she was most free of her inhibitions, as if only in bed could she express her true self, and only with a woman. Kay records my mother's confession of frigidity with my father and other men — including a rich but unstable Italian named Roberto she met when she was nineteen. Kay hints at misandry, but I think it was more likely fear or repulsion than hatred of men that led my mother into Kay's arms. It also suggested another plausible reason for her disastrous relationships with the opposite sex.

As well as instigating a new-found liberty, I can see why Kay appealed to my mother. Her fortissimo a counterpoint to my mother's femininity and grace, she was charismatic and gutsy and didn't give a toss for other people's opinions. They must have made a striking couple, blonde and brunette, robust and delicate, but they were opposites in more than looks.

When she met my mother, Kay and her long-term lover, the novelist Kathleen Farrell, were in the midst of one of their many separations. 'Kathleen was very pretty and fragile-looking,' Francis King said. 'She seemed conciliatory and appeared to go along with everything one said, but she had a will of her own. People thought that because Kay was so masculine she was the dominant one, but in fact it was Kathleen who was in charge.' Kay's bravado only worked on those who had little of their own. Like my father and Jean-Baptiste, she fitted my mother's criteria: the more troubled and volatile the better.

'Joan was Kay's type,' Raleigh Trevelyan added, 'but as she'd done with many other women, she used your mother to make Kathleen jealous.' This motive doesn't appear in *The Shelf*, where the author is the hesitant paramour, seduced by a persistent and beguiling younger woman. 'She was always the injured party looking to place the blame elsewhere,' Raleigh said. 'Joan was sweet and trusting, and Kay treated her very badly.

What happened with your mother was the last straw. After that I lost all respect for Kay.'

My father's friend Tony Curtis says of Kay: 'She was a larger than life character, in fact she was several novels in herself.' Along with extravagance and generosity, vengeance and paranoia were dominant features of her personality, and she took them to the page in *The Shelf*. Scores were settled with both friends and enemies for their real or imagined offences: Olivia Manning — known in literary circles as 'Olive Moaning' — is the hard-done-by and nosy novelist Sophia; a writer Kay calls Old Jawbones is her bête noire, the biographer Joanna Richardson; the cunning Carmelite priest is Father Brocard-Sewell of Allington Castle, my mother's confessor; and, superfluous to the plot, her next-door neighbours, with whom she battled on and off for years, are thoroughly belittled.

Kay also had it in for my father. Excising all trace of their former friendship, she all but emasculates him; as sexual predators, they'd undoubtedly slept with some of the same women, but here she's the sole contender. She paints him as a hopeless drunk and promiscuous homosexual; the words selfish and pathetic encapsulate her adjectival assassination. He was never a drinker, and as though his rumoured bisexuality might count as a cachet, she robs him of all appeal to women. My father *was* pathetic, in its saddest sense, but Kay fails to colour in any of the qualities that had earned him such popularity and respect from his peers. She wasn't among his visitors at Charing Cross Hospital, nor had she seen him in the five years since. If she had, she might have found a sliver of compassion for everything he'd lost, but it seems empathy wasn't within her gift.

My mother and I were living at Hyde Park Gardens during the four turbulent months of her relationship with Kay. In the novel, she refers to me as the child — at least I've progressed from the orphan — and glosses over my mother's maternal instincts, implying her feelings for me were perhaps ambivalent because I was a constant reminder of my father. Out of the way at Grandma's, I didn't complicate the storyline.

The letters continue to arrive, increasingly obsessive and their content often disquieting. Kay wrote only three in return, and reluctantly allows the affair to continue. The plot thickens when she suspects she has a rival, a married man who she views as conniving, untrustworthy, and none too attractive. My mother denies the accusation, saying he's merely a bothersome acquaintance who was once kind and helpful but of no interest to her. Kay doesn't believe her and calls her Calypso, the concealing goddess of the *Odyssey*.

A week before the affair was brought to an end, Kay records a chilling comment my mother made in one of her last letters: 'I've never had a future.' Despite her reservations, Kay depicts herself as an unlikely guardian and wonders whether she might have underestimated her own affections. Her reveries are interrupted when my father hires a private detective to trail my mother, claiming she's caught up in at least two affairs and unfit to look after me. Rather than stand her corner, my mother takes flight, leaving me with my grandparents. The conniving but kind married man finds himself in the role of chauffeur and diversionary tactic as they escape the city for an unnamed market town.

In her last letter to Kay, written the day after fleeing London, my mother says: 'I feel absolutely trapped . . . I'm not running away from you. Just running'; and in an unwitting symbolic act, following a visit to a local hairdresser: 'All my hair is cut short . . . I look like a shorn lamb ready for the slaughter.' A fugitive couple hiding out in an anonymous hotel in an unidentified town, the man signs the register Mr and Mrs — . My mother screens herself behind her sunglasses, as much a disguise as protection against the early September light.

On the run from my father and his detective, Kay's accusations and alternating attention and neglect, it seemed everyone wanted a piece of her, including me. For the time being, I was in safer hands than her own. Perhaps my father was right: she couldn't even take care of herself and was in no fit state to take care of me.

Off course and slowly falling into the murky depths, over a period of three days, the barbiturates in the bottle called out. It's said that the last stage of drowning is like the moment between the drift and the dream, so calm and peaceful it's hard to resist the final beckoning. I feel that's how it was for my mother. When she slipped into unconsciousness the married man panicked, called for an ambulance then sped away in his car, back to his wife. My mother died in hospital early the following morning. I've tried to write this sentence a hundred times but, just as when I was six, I still can't find the words.

Hidden under my mother's pillow in the hotel room were Kay's three love letters. A final, unposted letter to Kay was found in my mother's suitcase, the last line of which read: 'Hello darling and au revoir, I love you.' Kay doesn't believe it was an allusion to suicide

— my mother's faith would have prohibited it, and so would her passion for Kay. She also refuses to accept there was any sexual relationship with the unidentified man; it seems she didn't want to be seen as a cuckold.

No one is on trial here, but if anyone was accountable, censure died with my mother on 12 September 1962. None of the players could have altered her course. As unsure of herself and fearful as she was, it took me a long time to see that she always knew where she was heading.

★   ★   ★

When I first read *The Shelf*, I was disoriented by a plot I recognised and a mother more elusive than ever. Kay was a highly regarded author and the reviews were complimentary. Her friend Gillian Freeman called it a 'tour de force ... powerful in its evocation of relationships and the gradations of passion.' Elaine Feinstein wrote in *The Times*: 'This short fierce intelligent novel is as subtly accurate about the aphrodisiac effects of lesbian love as it is about the pain of loss.'

Thirteen years later, and no longer disoriented, I can't agree with the reviews. *The Shelf* is certainly short and fierce but I don't see much sign of 'the pain of loss', in fact Kay seems almost contemptuous of my mother's devotion. It's a cold little novel shot through with snobbery. The author casts herself as an avenging advocate pointing the finger at everyone else, including my grandparents who she upgrades to the bourgeois, bridge club set. As if she couldn't possibly be associated with an impoverished working class girl, she gives my mother a cultivated upbringing with a French education and a luxurious lifestyle funded by a private income. The facts are subtly, or not so subtly, contrived in Kay's favour and her callous gamesmanship conveyed as chivalry.

She was at work on *The Shelf* at least since 1965; a letter to Kay from Olivia Manning lodged at the University of Tulsa archives says that she hopes 'Suicide' is going well, and that it might be the breakthrough novel. It seems 'Suicide' was its working title. Olivia Manning died in 1980, four years before *The Shelf* was published, perhaps unaware that she was one of the thinly-disguised characters.

If Kay tried to find me to clear permission to quote from my mother's correspondence she didn't try very hard; until 1977 I was living at the same address that appears on the letters. I was only sixteen, but I'm certain my grandparents would have turned her request down flat; Kay was doubtless chief among the 'not nice' friends. I'm rather glad she chose to flout the copyright law, otherwise *The Shelf*'s intimate, if partial, portrait might have never been published.

★　★　★

My contact with Kay after we met in Brighton was intermittent, and she died before I discovered documented evidence of her gamesmanship. In his forthright obituary of Kay in the *Guardian*, Michael De-la-Noy wrote: 'For crudity, vulgarity and foul language Kay had few equals, yet, at her best, she could switch on genuine charm and offer useful encouragement to other writers. She exhibited an endearing kind of courage, even if you never knew when it would be your turn to be blasted out of your chair by a tirade of abuse.' Eventually I witnessed all the above.

In her professional and personal life, she could be a beast, but an entertaining and ostensibly generous one. She seemed unaware of her capacity to disappoint, but her small gifts might have been a subconscious plea for forgiveness, or a reminder of her presence. Penny Hoare, who edited *The Shelf*, said: 'I knew of Kay's reputation, and though I tried to keep our relationship on a formal level she often gave me presents, including a lithograph and a rose bush called Penelope, which still flowers every year in my garden.' There was always a pay-off with Kay, but real generosity takes a lot more than roses and book tokens.

In the *Oxford Dictionary of National Biography*, Peter Burton wrote: 'Neither a fluent nor a natural writer, Dick suffered throughout her career from writer's block and a fatal inability to meet deadlines.' It seems life got in the way of work, as well as principles. As Raleigh said, she had no scruples over the acquisition of money: 'I commissioned her to write a novel, but she took the same project to another publisher and received a second advance. The book was never written, and neither advance was paid back.' It happened more than once, but regardless of contractual obligations, she got away with it.

During her last decade Kay suffered a series of accidents and illnesses — a fractured shoulder, a punctured lung and pleurisy, among others. As her health declined she became even more ill-tempered and increasingly scathing of her ex-friends, and oddly disparaging of their sexuality. On the phone to me she dismissed one as 'a silly old poof' and another as 'that fucking queen'. She was also reluctant to tell me anything more about my mother. Foolhardy as I was, I continued to keep in touch, but whenever I tried to arrange a visit she would say, 'Call me in a few months when I'm feeling stronger.' When we last spoke, a year or so before she died, I'd interrupted her morning session with the radio. 'I'm listening to the fucking news,' she snapped, and hung up on me. As it was for so many others, my final encounter with Kay was barbed.

Towards the end, she alienated herself from all but a long-suffering coterie. Even Francis King, her close friend for over fifty years, was finally expelled from the club. He encouraged her ex-lover, Kathleen Farrell, to bequeath half her estate to Kay. When Kathleen died in 1999, she left Kay about £75,000, part of which she squandered on solicitor's fees. Paranoid to the last, she needed a closing round and found it in the wake of Kathleen's death. Infuriated over a secret clause in the will which instructed Sebastian Beaumont, one of the executors, to distribute various small possessions to Kathleen's friends, Kay accused him of a number of unfounded charges, including the withholding of certain items from her. Ever the diplomat, Francis suggested she was perhaps being a little unfair, with the result that she never spoke to him again.

Considering her treatment of him, Sebastian Beaumont is admirably gracious in his recollections of Kay: 'When she blew cold, she blew arctic but when she blew hot she was very warm indeed. She could be completely charming and flattering but when she was in a temper she was quite monstrous. I remember her once calling the local taxi rank she'd been using for years. She said, very imperiously, 'It's Kay Dick here, do you know who I am?' There was a short silence before she bellowed, 'Well fucking well get me someone who does!'' The altercation over the will was eventually settled in 2001, and she died shortly after from lung cancer.

We met only once but Kay made sure she left an impression, whereas my mother's seemed to fade as soon as she left the room. I was still grasping at air, but with the arrival of two packages, from Worcester and Brighton, my mother finally gave me her side of the story.

11

Forensic Evidence

My father's sensitivity and compassion had been paralysed by his suicide attempt. The little that was left functioning was as scrambled as his vocabulary. I doubt he was capable of mourning either my mother or a marriage motivated by necessity. With no thought for my grandparents' loss, he was more concerned with removing me from their custody. He wasn't invited to the funeral.

Grandma's nerves were already frayed from inherent anxiety and over-medication, but with the news of my mother's death they unravelled. During her breakdown her doctor ordered electroconvulsive therapy. Administered under general anaesthetic, ECT's controlled seizure caused temporary confusion and memory loss, side-effects that may or may not have contributed to the conspiracy of silence surrounding my mother's death.

I knew my mother had died in Worcester, Kay's unnamed market town, but I didn't understand why she was buried there with no one to visit her or bring flowers. Neither did the family in Wales, but it seems Cefn Cemetery in Merthyr was too close to home. 'We didn't know that Joan had died until about six weeks later when we read about it in one of the Sunday papers,' my Auntie Olwyn said. 'Your grandma told us that Joan was staying at a hotel in Worcester on her own. There was a dance going on downstairs and she couldn't sleep because of the noise. She said Joan had forgotten she'd already taken her sleeping pill, so she took another one. Apparently she died from an overdose of two pills. That was as much as we heard.' This was Grandma's story and she stuck with it, until she reworked it for me five years later.

Had my father's name not still been remembered, it's unlikely the press would have been interested. At Colindale Newspaper Library I searched through the Sunday papers from September to December 1962. After six hours of lurid headlines from the *Sunday Pictorial* to *The People*, I was informed that one microfilm reel from the period was missing. I'd put money on it that my mother's belated obituary appeared in the *Sunday Express*. In any case, the *Worcester Evening News* had run the story on 26 September, with the heading 'Woman Took Overdose of Drug'. Based on the evidence at the inquest, it was accurate up to a point. Worcester was only eighty miles from Merthyr, but luckily none of the relatives subscribed to its local paper.

Grandma's love of drama and disaster stopped short when the gossip turned in her direction. Hers was a respectable family and the unseemly details of my mother's death were swept under the nearest carpet. The taboo subjects for Grandma's generation included mental infirmity, illegitimacy, addiction and suicide. Our family had the lot. If Grandpa's Celtic sin was pride — the only thing he had left, having been stripped of status, decent wages and home — Grandma's equivalent virtue was prudence, her chary patchwork quilt a cover for disgrace.

It's said, on the quiet, that Wales has always been run by women. In the Welsh household the mother pulled the strings, or rather stage-managed the show, the stability and success of the children a testimony to her maternal qualities: public scandal was to be avoided at all costs. If Anne Howells had failed as a mother, no one was going to hear about it. When a child crossed the invisible line of propriety the whole family was shamed. My mother had well and truly crossed it, but the shame had to be redirected. With the married man, and of course Kay, cut from the cast list, my father took the lead as the villain. The bit players, including the Crazy Count and a chorus of nameless boyfriends, remained in the wings. By curtain-up, the tragedy had been rewritten: as Olwyn said, 'With Auntie Anne, you always had to read between the lines.' I understand why Grandma couldn't tell me the truth about my mother's death but it's left me with an aversion for travesty.

I was about seven when she told me my mother died of cancer. En route to Merthyr, we went to visit her grave. It was covered in little green rocks that looked like emeralds. I took one of them home with me and kept it in the pocket of my school blazer. Eventually it disappeared, but I don't remember losing it, just as I don't remember losing my mother. In the thirty-five years since, I've often thought about visiting her grave again and wondered if the green rocks had been washed away by the rain, but something held me back. I was waiting for the right moment.

Over the years my perspective on my parents shifted from childhood detachment and teenage indifference to the tentative curiosity of my late twenties when my cousin on the wrong side of the family let slip that my father hadn't died of pneumonia, he'd overdosed on sleeping pills. This was the first of two revelations I put aside until I was ready to face them.

It's easy to lose track of family secrets; like an album of blurred black and white photos, with the 'not nice' scissored out, no one wants to flick through it. Tidied away in a safe place and left to gather dust, after a while everyone forgets where it's hidden. The only real conversation about my mother I ever had with Gomez occurred in 1989, eight years before I finally walked away from Castle Greyskull without a backward glance. He said he was shocked that I didn't know how she died, but with Gomez it was always hard to distinguish the disclaimer from the expedient elision. It seems no one had thought to tell me. Grandma had died in 1981, Grandpa couldn't have found the words, so it was left to Gomez — and therefore left. The exchange lasted no more than ten minutes, throughout which I squirmed with discomfort as he tried to weasel his way around the specifics; we didn't do overt emotion, yet this story demanded it. I wish I'd heard it from someone else. A year or so later I did, in more vivid but equally biased detail when I read *The Shelf*. In a rare moment of partial candour, Gomez ran through my mother's Last Act, though his cast list was a bit short too.

★ ★ ★

As I approached forty, solvent, freelance, but once again single, I realised the lacunae in my past were draining me of solace in the present. I'd had enough of sidestepping my parents' shadows. My discoveries provoked intense and unexpected reactions, including compassion, delight, disbelief and exasperation, but there was one emotion missing. It was buried so deep I couldn't reach it.

I'm only now aware that I was following a subconscious sequence of research, and I postponed one particular enquiry until I had supporting evidence. Two years ago, I called the coroners' offices in Worcester and Westminster requesting the files on my parents' deaths. I was told that the archives from the 1960s were incomplete since records were periodically destroyed due to lack of space. They said they'd be in touch if they found them. Weeks passed and I prepared myself for disappointment.

On a Saturday afternoon in September, I received a phone call from a Mrs Pamela Round. She sounded breathless, as if she'd just raced up a flight of stairs. 'I hope you don't mind me calling you at the weekend, but I thought you'd want to know I've just found the information you requested about

278

your mother, and it's a very big file.

'I'm skimming through it and it's all here like a documentary. You'll know what your mother had for lunch, where she got her prescriptions and even where she bought her groceries.' I heard her turning pages. 'There are a lot of witness statements here, and . . . ' She stopped mid sentence. 'I've just realised, you were only a baby — ' She was unable to say 'when your mother died'. I've lived with the story my whole life and I often forget how distressing it is to other people.

'By the way,' she said, 'there's a letter here from your mother to a Miss Kay Dick of Hampstead. It's a bit torn but quite legible.' Kay wrote in *The Shelf* that she hadn't attended the inquest but had conducted her own investigation with the help of the coroner's officer, who returned to her the three letters found under my mother's pillow. The final letter was evidence, but he'd given Kay a typed copy of it.

The next two days passed slowly. By Tuesday morning I was unable to sit still for more than a few seconds. When I heard the post thud on the doormat, the breath caught in my throat: I was about to relive my mother's last few days. I held the A4 envelope in my hands for a moment, feeling anxious and edgy, but also scared that I might find what I'd been searching for — or, worse, that I might not. I'd thought my mother's letter to Kay would be my first priority, and when I opened the envelope there it was, a small pale blue page torn to pieces and Sellotaped together. It began 'Darling'. I wasn't quite ready to read my mother's last written words and I placed the letter to one side.

I read through the next thirty-three pages without pausing. In contrast to the eloquence and articulacy of my parents' friends the language was pedestrian, the grammar ungainly and as cluttered as real life. The first statement was from my mother's younger brother. Despite my feelings for Gomez I felt a flicker of sympathy as I read the first line of his statement: 'I am twenty-one years of age.' He said he had identified his sister's body at 3.10 p.m. on 10 September 1962. I'd got the date of her death wrong by two days; it was the first of many errors corrected. 'Her faculties were good but she had never been a robust person and in recent months she had lost weight and appeared to be worried, but I had not known her to have any bouts of serious depression.' It sounded as though Gomez anticipated the question of suicide since it was obvious my mother wasn't only depressed but desperate.

The next statement was from PC Henry

Venn: 'I caused enquiries to be made by the Metropolitan Police in order to estimate the number of Nembutal capsules which could have been available to the deceased. A number of chemists were interviewed and it was ascertained that during the period 21 May 1962 to 3 September 1962, a total of 650 Nembutal capsules had been issued on prescriptions bearing the deceased's name.' He went on to say my mother was registered with at least four different doctors in Kent and London, that the police were unable to trace all the prescriptions, and of the 650 capsules, 110 had been dispensed between 29 August and 3 September.

I didn't recognise the name on the next statement, a Bentley Middleton of Chart Sutton: 'I have been told by PC Hesketh that I am not obliged to say anything unless I wish to do so, but anything I say may be given in evidence.' The declaration belonged to the married man who had abandoned my mother. The name conjured up a smooth and brilliantined Terry-Thomas bounder, but Bentley was neither smooth nor brilliant, as his ten-page statement revealed. 'I have known Joan Swan for the past twelve months. The village is a small one and our families became friendly.' Bentley and his wife ran the grocery store and Post Office — ' . . . in

December of 1961 things became rather strained between Joan and her husband. His wife was also a writer and was working for the BBC at the time, and was keeping the family. She was earning £15.15s. per week.' This sounded like an odd detail for a friendly neighbourhood grocer to know and one of many Bentley would let slip, including the fact that he first gave his name to the police as Mr Swan.

After my mother and I moved in with my grandparents, he said: 'When in London I used to visit her occasionally. Sometimes she appeared to be very low and depressed.' On the second page of his statement, he repeats that she was 'very low' four times, as if setting the scene for the coroner. In August that year my mother told Bentley she was going to Paris with her sister, Susan, for a couple of weeks. 'I was surprised to learn that Joan had returned from Paris early. Later Joan told me that she had come home on account of a woman called Kay Dick. Joan told me Kay was in the habit of sending her bunches of roses. I formed the opinion that this association was an unhealthy one. The woman Kay Dick appeared to have a hold over Joan and this appeared to distress her.' The euphemism 'unhealthy' jumped off the page, as did Kay sending roses: it seems the relationship wasn't quite as one-sided as she claimed.

On Sunday, 2 September, Bentley telephoned my mother to say he was going to Worcester the following Tuesday to visit a relative. 'Joan told me that she was going to Cornwall for a month with a friend named Kathy. She asked me if I would call and see her before she went as she had something important to see me about. On Tuesday Joan said, 'Kathy's got to go to Italy and our holiday is off for the time being.' Joan wanted to come with me to Worcester . . . she begged me to take her with me saying, 'Please I beg of you to take me out of London.' At this time she was very distressed and crying.'

On the way to Worcester, they stopped in Oxford and booked into a hotel. 'She suggested that we had single beds and if we could only book a double bed perhaps I could sleep on the floor. I rang my wife to tell her where I was. I told her that Joan was coming along with me for a ride. I took two pillows and the eiderdown and slept at the foot of the bed.'

When they arrived at the Talbot Hotel in Worcester the following day, Bentley goes through the same motions: 'I slept on the floor and Joan slept in the bed. I woke up the next morning and Joan told me she didn't feel too well. In the afternoon Joan went up and layed on the bed and was reading. At about 5 p.m. I left to buy Joan a packet of Salem cigarettes. I returned at about 6 p.m.'

At about 10.30 p.m., 'Joan was still in bed and appeared very drowsy. I shook her but she didn't wake up. It was then I realised something was wrong.' He asked the hotel landlady to help him and then called for an ambulance. 'The doctor and ambulance men gave Mrs Swan medical attention, and when they moved Mrs Swan, three letters were found underneath her pillow.' He followed the ambulance to Worcester Royal Infirmary and waited in the Casualty Department until about 1.30 a.m., when he was told there was nothing more he could do: 'So I decided to go home, hoping Joan would be all right.' The next day he rang the hospital three times: 'I was told that Joan was critically ill. [The following morning] I again rang and was told that Joan had passed away at 6.30 a.m.'

In a second brief statement Bentley said: 'Joan had told me that her husband had suggested to her on two occasions that they should both commit suicide and end it all.' As shocking as it was, I had the feeling he was telling the truth. His wife, Amelia, backed him up; 'On 7 August 1962, Joan Swan telephoned at 2 p.m. I asked how she was, she

284

replied in her usual way, 'So, so, you know.' She then added as a sort of afterthought, 'Other than committing suicide.'' It seemed suspicious that Mrs Middleton would have remembered the date and time of the phone call; perhaps like her husband she was scene-setting for the coroner.

The hotel landlady, Grace Armstrong, threw a spanner in the works when she said: 'The man signed the book in the name of Mr and Mrs J. Swan, of Hyde Park Gardens, London. The woman was very well dressed and wearing dark glasses. It was very obvious she did not want to be recognised.' Of the evening in question, Mrs Armstrong said: 'Later the man said, 'My wife is very ill.' After dialling 999 he said, 'I never thought it would come to this.''

The final statement was my father's, given three days after my mother died. He had little to hide by this point and said that my mother had tried to commit suicide at least twice before, the first time while she was living in South Africa. Towards the end of their marriage he said: 'She began to get very depressed and bad tempered. Two weeks after my wife had left me she told me that Bentley Middleton had been coming up to London to see her. I questioned Middleton about this and he agreed that he had been seeing my wife in London. Shortly after she had left I received a telegram which stated, 'Joan loves Bentley, signed Christine.' I believe it was my wife who sent it, probably while she was under the influence of drugs.' A note from a PC Hare indicates the difficulties of obtaining this statement, part-written in my father's left-handed scrawl, part-spoken in fractured sentences and typed up by the constable.

At the inquest held on 20 September, the coroner's verdict was 'Accidental overdose of Pentobarbitone'. The final page of the report was a request from the Forensic Science Laboratory: 'Please give authority for the destruction of the organs in our possession.' Until then the one image I'd avoided was the post-mortem: my mother's body lying on the pathologist's slab, the ugly Y-shaped incision and her organs removed for analysis. The thought of her in pieces is harrowing, but the knowledge that her heart was destroyed in a hospital incinerator feels like a desecration.

It wasn't until I turned to my mother's torn letter that I noticed an omission in the report: there was no statement from Kay. I can only assume that the coroner thought the situation indelicate. As she did so frequently, Kay had the last word, her novel standing as both accusation and defence.

My mother's letter was written five days

before she died. It reminded me of the passing comment she'd made about love letters in the *Listener* column: 'a glimpse of the personality behind the pen — the private individual committing to paper words from the heart, intended only for the recipient, not for the public'. I recognised several lines lifted word for word in *The Shelf*: 'I feel absolutely trapped . . . I almost sense something awful.' And after she'd cut off her hair she did indeed say: 'I look like a shorn lamb ready for the slaughter.' The last line was: 'Hello darling and au revoir. I love you.'

In a daze, I replaced the pages in their envelope: I'd found what I'd been looking for but I couldn't take in all this raw information, let alone place it in any kind of order. Fortunately, I had a deadline to meet. I was editing a dry and monotonous corporate report, but the tedium was never more welcome. The rest of the day is a blur, but I remember catching sight of my face in the mirror: wide-eyed, my skin pale and glassy, I looked as though I'd just walked away from a car crash. It was the end of September but my flat felt as cold as mid winter. I turned the heating up but I couldn't get warm.

I went to bed just after midnight, my thoughts spinning and colliding. At about 2 a.m. I leaped out of bed. I made a cup of tea but again unable to sit still, I paced the living room carpet. My mother was caught up in two affairs, one a convenience, the other all-consuming. She'd just come back from Paris and was planning a trip to Cornwall. Her addiction was out of control and the drugs were her first priority. Throughout the thirty-three page report, there were only two cursory references to me, as if I were an afterthought: by the way, it seemed to say, there was a baby around somewhere. Where did I fit in? I kept coming back to the same answer: I didn't. No wonder I couldn't find my place in this story.

Bentley had also said my father had hit my mother more than once, but his suggestion that they should commit suicide together sickened me. I'll never know whether it happened before or after I was born, or even when my mother was pregnant, but either way it was a proposal of murder.

A friend once asked me a question I didn't understand at the time: 'Why aren't you angry at your parents?' The question seemed ridiculous: they were dead, why would I be angry at them? On the surface all seemed calm, but my subconscious was apparently apoplectic.

I tried to write down my thoughts, but every few sentences I jumped up from my desk, throwing my pen across the room. I may have punched the wall a couple of times. The pages are illegible and barely coherent, but I can just make out the words 'selfish', 'disgraceful' and 'irresponsible', punctuated with a lot of swear words. Until that night I'd always made excuses for my parents' actions and the one worn ragged with overuse was: 'They couldn't help it.' The alternative was too painful to contemplate. Now I know why I don't have any self-pity — my parents used it all up. I went back to bed at dawn and slept like a baby. The next day I turned their photographs face down: I couldn't bear to look at them.

★   ★   ★

The coroner's report into my father's death arrived two days later, but by then I was running short on sympathy. I read through the ten pages with as much deliberation as I would an AGM accounting from my building society. It held no surprises. The Westminster coroner was blunt in his conclusion: 'Barbiturate poisoning. Killed himself.' Fair enough, I thought.

Anger stayed close by me for the next three weeks or so. Then, having served its purpose, it vanished as swiftly as it arrived. It didn't disappear completely, but for now it had found a still and contained place and I knew it would be there when I needed it.

A couple of months went by before I read my father's report again. He was found by a neighbour on the morning of 30 December 1967, an empty glass of beer and a bottle of Nembutal by his bedside. The landlord said: 'He was a quiet man and didn't mix with the other tenants.' By now he'd cut himself off from everyone, but especially his literary friends. Francis King and Raleigh Trevelyan told me when they ran into my father he turned his face away and crossed the road to avoid them, as he'd done with Dylan Thomas nearly twenty years earlier. As if he couldn't bear his friends to witness his self-destruction, he was ducking into his own doorway.

My father died on 30 December, unable to face another New Year. His funeral was held at Golders Green Crematorium. 'It's one of my saddest memories,' his sister Pauline said. 'He'd known everyone in the publishing world, but there were only a handful of people there.' Until *The Times* ran his obituary on 3 January, none of his former inner circle — including Francis, Raleigh, John Lehmann, Hamish Hamilton, Iliana and Maurice Cranston, Terence Cooper and, of course, Margot Walmsley — knew he was dead.

My father didn't write a will, let alone

appoint a literary executor. He had nothing to leave, except the books he'd written, but I wondered what had happened to his correspondence with Somerset Maugham, Max Beerbohm, Angus Wilson and all his other literary friends. Most of all I wondered about his journal, which several people had mentioned. I eventually discovered that when Pauline had cleared his bed-sit, aside from a few photographs, she threw everything out, including the journal. I have all his books but at least I can stop looking for his letters and papers, along with my mother's missing manuscript, disintegrating as they are at the bottom of a landfill site.

The coroner's report also contained a letter from his oldest sister Vera, who had fallen out with their brother John over his attitude towards my father. They were communicating through solicitors after John had offered my father financial assistance 'on the understanding that Dr Swan will be accorded complete and unfettered responsibility without opposition or intervention'. Vera wrote that my father was a proud and dignified man and refused John's proposition 'after he overheard his brother say that he would not allow him into his house'.

My eyes filled with tears when I realised how alone my father was. It was the first time

I'd ever cried for him as I remembered his bare and chilly bed-sit in Shepherd's Bush, a worn armchair and an electric fire the only concessions to comfort. The air smelled of winter, as if the dust had turned to ice crystals. His silk cravat kept him warm but it also hid the scar across his throat, as did his beard; or perhaps he didn't trust himself to shave with his shaky left hand. More likely, he didn't trust himself with a razor. As a young man he'd been well-groomed and smartly-dressed, taking care of his physique as well as his stylish wardrobe. During his last decade, his gait hampered by paralysis, he'd gained about three stone. At forty-four, he was a shuffling, mumbling wreck in a tattered shirt and a shabby raincoat.

For my seventh birthday, on 18 December, he'd given me the dictionary I'd flipped through for hours on end, minting new words for my collection. Twelve days later he was dead. It was probably the last time I saw him. Vera's letter also said one of the last things he did was to put my name down for Christ's Hospital. Although he wouldn't be here to see it, my father was thinking of my future.

The coroners' reports told me more than I'd hoped for, but there were a few questions they couldn't answer, such as: is there ever a positive aspect to suicide? It brings a release from suffering, an end to pain and, perhaps most surprising of all, a fundamental dignity. When your sole choice is self-murder, I can only imagine it's a lucid and logical decision taken with absolute determination. This is when an open verdict is the final insult. It saves family and friends from culpability but demeans the deceased's last sovereign act. Neither of my parents left a note, yet the verdict in my mother's inquest allowed her a Catholic burial and my grandparents to interpret her death as an accident, even though she'd made at least two previous attempts on her life. My father's pre-history left no doubt in the Westminster coroner's outcome. I can't help but think there was more respect in the latter's conclusion.

I had one last question: I needed to know how many pills my parents had taken. The pathology results were impossible to translate into layman's terms: my mother's read 'a high blood level of barbiturate, 3 mg%', and my father's 'blood barbiturate estimation — 1.4 mgs%'. I asked his school friend Michael Gribble, a retired pathologist, for help. As well as explaining the medical terminology, he calculated that my father had taken nine pills, my mother eighteen. The recommended dosage for Nembutal was no more than two. I had my answer.

As if an evidential dam had burst open, within the month another witness appeared when I received a letter from a woman named Jane Goff: 'You won't remember me,' she wrote, 'but I lived next door to your parents in Chart Sutton in 1961.' Like Dot Barclay, Jane had seen the article in the *Mail on Sunday*. Over lunch in a village pub in Kent, she filled me in on the last six months of my parents' marriage.

'Joan would wander over to our kitchen in the mornings for a cup of tea and a chat. She seemed to be in a haze and never really came to until midday.' Jane couldn't figure out where I was and who was taking care of me. I've since discovered that various people looked after me when my mother couldn't cope, such as neighbours — including Bentley Middleton's wife — a friend in London and my grandparents.

'Late at night your father often stood outside our house wearing his silk dressing gown and throwing gravel at the upstairs window to wake us up,' Jane said. 'I'd run over to the cottage where your mother was in a terrible state, hysterical and whimpering like a wounded animal. The only time I ever saw you cry was when they were fighting, which was usually at around one in the morning. You were screaming in your cot in the next room and I'd pick you up and rock you back to sleep.' It seems my mother had a few symptoms in common with her first husband, Jean-Baptiste: 'One minute she'd be sobbing and distraught, the next right as rain. It was most peculiar, and usually only happened when I said I'd call for the doctor.'

Jane remembered my mother telling her how my father proposed. A few weeks after they met, she was reading aloud to him in the garden at Allington Castle when he stopped her at certain words, spelling out the sentence: Will you marry me? 'It makes you think of a Mills and Boon version of Tristan and Isolde,' Jane said, 'as though their whole relationship was coloured by tragic romance.'

Jane and her family called my father's fractured speech Swanese: 'You had to grasp his meaning from two or three words out of every ten. One night, we heard the gravel at the window and your father shouting from the driveway, 'Gun, gun.' I ran to the cottage thinking he'd shot her, but he meant 'gone.' I think that was when your mother left him for good.

'Bentley was an amiable and nice enough man,' Jane said, 'but I can't imagine what your mother saw in him.' Apparently he was more Sid James than Terry-Thomas. Blind as my father was to the gradations between ugliness and beauty, but well aware of social standing, he would have been horrified that he'd been traded for a grocer. Once again he'd lost out to a rival he saw as vulgar and unattractive, yet in his way Bentley had a lot more to offer than my father. 'Joan was desperate for support and affection,' Jane said. 'I think she was grateful, more than anything, that Bentley was so kind and generous to her.' He didn't charge her for the groceries she ordered, which only fuelled the rumours in the village.

When I sent Jane the coroners' reports, she was on the case like Miss Marple, analysing the statements and weighing up the evidence. 'It's all terribly fishy and unresolved. I think the coroner must have been either very considerate or a bit priggish, since your mother's affairs with Bentley and Kay barely figure in the report.' Jane wasn't asked to give a statement, but unlike Kay she would have proved an expert witness.

A few weeks later, substantiating evidence arrived in the post when Kay's executors kindly sent me my mother's love letters. There were fourteen in all. A keen archivist of her own papers, Kay had not only dated and numbered them, she'd also jotted notes in the margins.

Written in my mother's swiftly scrawled hand — no pseudonym, no hiding behind her husband's name — I tried to read her letters aloud. It was the closest I would get to hearing her voice, but I managed only two or three paragraphs before my own voice wavered and eventually stalled. As she said in the *Listener*: 'There is usually a spontaneity in the letter-form which releases any inhibitions and one feels free to confess on paper what one would normally conceal in speech.' She concealed nothing as she laid bare a woman pleading for love and stripped of all self-respect. If anything, Kay underplayed my mother's obsession.

She confirmed that a private detective was following her, and that my father had tried to kick down the door of my grandparents' flat during one of several attempts to kidnap me. Now I understood why I'd felt such a visceral fear of abduction as an eight-year-old. She also wrote that she was suffocating at home and eager to move out: 'My parents were away for a whole week which was bliss! Now it's all hell once again.' The most distressing were written at around 4.30 a.m. in a fog of barbiturate excess. One contains a reference to suicide: 'Right this moment I couldn't care if tomorrow never comes. Such is life. No wonder people think they are free to end it all.' Her letters corroborate 95 per cent of *The Shelf*; the final 5 per cent is neither here nor there, such as the changing of names and elevating of background and Bentley's line of work.

In one of her most personal *Listener* columns my mother quoted Hazlitt: 'The dupe of friendship, and the fool of love; have I not reason to hate and to despise myself?' Diffidence and self-doubt were written plain in her professional correspondence as well as her love letters, as if inviting the recipient to respond with the inevitable reproach or rejection. As for her feelings for Kay, I burned with humiliation on her behalf and I can't bring myself to expose her as Kay did in *The Shelf*. My mother was unable to protect herself or her dignity, but it's the least I can do.

Grandpa once told me, quite matter-of-factly, that he saw my mother's ghost every now and then. Unacquainted with the customs of the spirit world, I asked if she talked to him. 'Of course she didn't,' he said, 'don't be so daft.' Apparently itinerant souls, even if bound to silence, will happily visit to check on loved ones.

After reading her letters, I dreamed about my mother for the first time that night. She stopped by to see me after one of her trips abroad. We sat on the sofa in my living room, the contents of her suitcase in disarray at our feet. Our toenails were polished the same fuchsia pink and it seemed perfectly natural that she was younger than me. I didn't ask where she'd been or why it had taken her so long to come and see me; she was here and that was enough. Breaking with paranormal convention, she talked non-stop while I tried to listen. I remember nothing of her conversation, but the sound and sight of her lingers, along with the scent of lemon zest and lavender.

Her voice was soft but strong and her hands danced in the air as she talked. She was fizzing with delight and laughter. With her gleaming auburn hair, bright blue eyes and tanned, flawless skin, she was vibrant and assured, but most of all at ease. This was the woman she might have been, who wouldn't have looked twice at Bentley, didn't need pills to get through the day and would never have pleaded for love from anyone. After about twenty minutes, she stood up and I watched her cross the living room. She paused at the door and blew me a kiss. 'I'll be back in a minute, sweetheart,' she said. I curled up on the sofa and waited for her. When I woke up, she'd gone. Most of my dreams disintegrate within moments of waking, but I'm holding on to this one. It may not be real, but it's the only memory I have of her.

★ ★ ★

Seven months had passed since I read the coroners' reports. As the information settled I realised why I'd waited so long to visit my mother: I needed to find out for myself who she really was. There were still a few gaps in the story, but for now they could wait.

On her birthday, 23 April, in the shade of an oak tree at Astwood Cemetery in Worcester, I sat beside her grave. It looked neglected and I tidied it as best I could. Clearing aside the dead leaves with my hands, the last trace of anger washed away by big, hot tears, I saw hundreds of little green rocks. I have one in my pocket as I write.

12

Absent Parents

Some of us are lucky, or unlucky, enough to experience the grand passion, the once-in-a-lifetime love against which we measure all other joys and sorrows. When my parents found theirs it destroyed them. Mine might have done the same had I not followed a different path.

From an early age, I was fiercely independent and self-contained, stubborn in my resolve to show what I was made of; having turned my nose up at the 'abandoned' banner, I wore my so-called bravery like a badge of honour, unwittingly loyal to the Hyde family motto 'Soyez Ferme'. *Fermé*, however, means closed. As an adult, these traits proved to be both assets and liabilities; my Achilles' heel was the unyielding belief that the only person I could trust to take care of me was myself. I was still the tough little girl in ankle socks, facing life's setbacks as though they were adventures.

I had little to confirm it, yet I'd told myself I was nothing like my parents. Too eager to flag the differences and deny the similarities, when I began investigating their lives I was appalled to find I was repeating one of their most significant mistakes. With one or two exceptions, my love life was almost as messy as theirs: I was drawn to doomed relationships that end in unnecessary pain and heartache. It seemed I'd inherited more than my father's blue eyes and my mother's insomnia.

When genuine love came knocking I couldn't answer the door. Andy and I were together for four years. He looked after me through surgery, changed my bandages when my scar became infected and kept watch over me as I slowly healed. He was there beside me at every hospital appointment, devoted and dependable, the kind of man who would never let you down. These were aspects so unfamiliar and therefore uncomfortable that his love left me bewildered and with a heart locked shut. No one could get close enough to glimpse let alone touch my vulnerability, not even Andy.

The night we broke up we talked until dawn. I owned up to my fears and frailties and unleashed a few of the grubbier family secrets. When I told him what Morticia and Gomez had done when I was eighteen, I realised I'd kept quiet out of unwarranted loyalty and gratuitous shame: it was hard to admit but I was deeply ashamed of my own relatives and the silent seething they sanctioned. It was the first time I'd talked about it in twenty years and it was the first time Andy saw me cry. That night I unpinned my badge from my lapel. Like the old coat that still fits but doesn't suit you any more, it had to go. I was thirty-eight and finally equipped to confront the childhood disadvantages I'd been avoiding my whole life.

★ ★ ★

Over the next two years I sorted my way through the ancestral closet and threw out what I no longer needed. For now I had to do it alone, but as if they'd been waiting for the right moment, the gods who had compensated me for my inauspicious start set me one last challenge. As the seeds of this book were sown I fell in love with a man who was brilliant, sensitive, prone to black moods and above all unavailable. I'd found the grand passion that brings more sorrow than joy.

We met at a mutual friend's party in Kensington. J. was tall and lean and a bit scruffy round the edges, as if he hadn't been clothes-shopping since 1985. His shirt was frayed at the collar and missing a button or two and the hems of his trousers were turned up on the outside. Something about those hems touched me and I wanted to sew them for him. He looked like a six foot one lost boy in need of a playmate. I didn't know it at the time but his childhood wasn't so different from mine and in many ways his loss was harder to bear.

J. did a good job of presenting an invincible front but his eyes gave him away; they were as dark as burned chestnuts and as wary as a fox on Boxing Day. In company he often looked at me for reassurance, or to make sure I was still there. Since I have to disguise his identity I can't disclose his story but, as an only child, he carried it alone and with fortitude although at a great cost; his wariness keeps him watchful and isolated.

Three days after we met, I ran into him at a second-hand bookshop on Charing Cross Road. I'd just found a copy of the 1949 edition of Henry James' *A Little Tour in France*. When I said my father had written the introduction, J. insisted on buying it for me. We went for a coffee at an Italian café on Old Compton Street and I told him a story I'd recently heard from my godmother. When I was a toddler, my father used to talk of our travelling around Europe together when I reached eighteen, 'presenting' me to the landed gentry and wealthy expats he'd met as a young man. I was to be dressed in exquisite frocks with exotic flowers in my hair. He had visions of my being courted by an Italian aristocrat, with a castello in the Tuscan hills and a villa in Florence. Eventually we would both reap the benefits of a well-connected marriage. It was Henry James and his protégé at their most aspirational — displaced aesthetes peering through the keyhole to catch what the duchess is saying. It was also a perfect illustration of my father's state of mind.

His Jamesian fantasy would have fallen short on several counts. At eighteen, I was a child of the late 1970s, likely to be dressed in a black leather mini-skirt and a Sex Pistols T-shirt, though I did occasionally wear a pink carnation in my hair. My cultural pursuits at that time would have horrified my father: punk and ska, Kurt Vonnegut novels and Marvel comic books. He'd envisaged my dazzling conversation and charming personality compensating for his faltering speech and morose manner. At that age I neither dazzled nor charmed in adult company; I was gauche, tongue-tied and frequently blushed when addressed by a grown-up. We would have made a right pair.

Over cappuccino and cannolo, J. and I

skipped the small talk as he asked all sorts of penetrating questions that might have unsettled me coming from anyone else. I told him things I wouldn't normally share with a stranger; we already had an implicit short cut to intimacy. Most of all, he wanted to know why I wasn't a total basket-case. No one else had phrased it quite so directly. Leaning across the Formica table, I said, 'Maybe it's my belated rebellion against my parents.' He reached out and held my hand, nodding as if he understood without my having to explain. We were about as close as two people can get without kissing. I wouldn't hear his story for some time yet, but in unburdening mine I sensed a familiar trait: he was a good listener.

Aside from my father, J. was the only person who called me by my full name, Anna-Petra. A few weeks later, we were rushing for the last train at Green Park Tube and I was striding ahead of him. In his gabardine raincoat, he touched my arm and did a shuffling little dance that stopped me short; he reminded me of my father, all the way down to his big scuffed shoes.

In the most precarious of circumstances, for the first time in my life I felt safe; in fact, I felt as though I'd come home. J. was both present and absent and as caught up in the story as my parents. During the next four years our affair was more off than on, and every time he left it felt like a death I had to mourn all over again. I didn't know how to let go and neither did J. In thrall to our interrupted childhoods, we were selfish, reckless and greedy, to say nothing of guilty. It ended six months ago, but neither of us could find a way to say goodbye.

★　★　★

Every now and then, since my late teens, I was overwhelmed by a sadness so deep it hurt to breathe. I knew where it came from but I couldn't quite give it a name, as though bestowing it with a title might make it worse and that if I gave in to it too often it might never leave me. Intermittent as it was, it was easy enough to bury. The sadness, however, was missing a counterpart emotion.

Until I read the coroners' reports I'd always thought anger was destructive and hateful and to be avoided at all costs. It reminded me of my father and Gomez, and whenever a man shouted at me I regressed to the mute five-year-old on the steps of the British Museum or the incoherent teenager packing her carrier bags. Having missed out on almost every stage of the parent-child relationship, but most of all, as I'd admitted to J., the teenage rebellion, I could neither defy nor dismay my parents, nor could I shout, 'I hate you! I wish you were dead!' More importantly, I'd bypassed the earlier grieving process and one of its most crucial phases — anger. Mine was misdirected: I'd had to make do with Morticia and Gomez, who were poor substitutes whichever way I look at it.

Now that I'd found the missing emotion I had no idea how to deal with it, until my friend Tom let me in on it. He was always on the move, driven, speedy and running late, as if he were on a permanent adrenaline high. He suppressed his anger as well as I did. That day he looked different: calm, contented — and on time. 'What happened?' I asked. When he told me he'd just been on an anger management course I knew what my next move was.

With the assurance from Tom that it wasn't at all New Agey tree hugging and yoghurt weaving, I signed up for the same course. It was run by Mike Fisher, a charismatic, forthright South African. As an angry man himself, he knows his subject inside out. There were ten of us on the course, and not a tree hugger in sight. Our stories were different but we were all there for the same reason. Everyone looked a bit startled and uneasy, not knowing what to expect but certain at some point we'd have to come clean.

Many of the concepts were logical and easily grasped, others were complicated, to say nothing of painful. 'Conflict Resolution' and 'Clearing' were straightforward, but the phrase 'rage is frozen shame' took a little longer to assimilate, until Mike went on to explain the fear of exposure that comes with it. I've met with shame in all its colours throughout the writing of this book. At times I felt as though I were flipping up my skirt and showing my knickers, until a (male) friend said, 'Anna, come on — we want to see your knickers but we don't want you to take them off.' The image made me realise that a glimpse of lace is fine, and if occasionally your elastic snaps and your drawers fall to your ankles in public, that's okay too.

The most relevant and complex concept Mike introduced us to was 'Shadows', the murky hues we choose not to see, that we hide, repress or deny: they're the triggers for anger that wound like a dagger to the heart. However, when you hold your shadow in front of you, look it in the face and give it a good talking to, you *own* it and it no longer owns you. Until that moment I'd had no idea how to approach let alone negotiate with my shadows. When I told the class the title of my book, a collective gasp went round the room.

I had the feeling there would be a catharsis at some point and that it would be me who would bring it about. Both dreading and hoping for it, I bided my time. Over the next two days I trickled information: my parents had died when I was very young: I was brought up by my grandparents; and I had only recently discovered the truth about my parents' deaths. On the last day of the course, a phrase came up that set the catharsis in motion.

Mike began talking about emotional vampires, the people in our lives who we allow to drain us of strength and determination. When he said the only solution is to walk away from them and not look back, I started crying and couldn't stop. I briefly explained my relationship with J., but I knew I was really talking about my parents. When I said they'd killed themselves, I was a blubbering mess, choking on my words as I tried to say that J. had got caught up in it and I couldn't separate him from my parents. Mike got it in one when he said, 'You're addicted to yearning.' The moment he identified it, the noise that came out of me was primal, like a

310

prehistoric creature buried so deep it had to howl with all its might to drag itself out of its pit. Mike stopped the class. He asked me to choose two people to play my mother and father. I chose Isabel and Ian, in part because I knew they both had children.

Once I'd placed the three of us on the sofa, Mike said, 'Go ahead, Anna. Your mother is right there beside you. Talk to her.' I felt self-conscious and silly, sitting on a sofa in a big house in the Surrey countryside pretending to talk to my parents. I started to speak and within seconds I felt everyone in the room but Isabel and Ian vanish. I held Isabel's hands and tried to say 'Mummy', but I stumbled over it: it still felt awkward and borrowed. Eventually the one question I could never find the words for as a six-year-old finally came out: 'How could you leave me?'

Isabel gripped my arms and pulled me towards her. As she spoke, her voice was soft but forceful and her big brown eyes turned bright blue: 'Sweetheart, I had to leave you . . . I couldn't take care of you the way you needed me to . . . my life was unbearable and I couldn't take any more pain . . . I was suffering and so were you but I knew I was leaving you in safer hands than mine . . . Darling, I left you because I loved you too much to hurt you any more.' When she'd said what I needed to hear, she squeezed me close and stroked my hair as I cried on her shoulder. Her arms felt warm and safe: at that moment, I was her first priority and she wasn't going anywhere.

When Mike asked me to talk to my father I didn't know what I wanted to say, but when it came out it astonished both of us. As I stroked Ian's hand I said, 'I'm so sorry I didn't love you, but when you shouted at me you frightened me . . . I think you killed yourself because I didn't love you.' Ian looked stunned, his lip trembling as he shook his head: 'I never meant to frighten you . . . I'm sorry I made you feel so scared . . . you were so little and I never meant to hurt you but I didn't know what I was doing.' Ian knew nothing of my father's rage and frustration, nor of his inability to communicate, yet somehow he'd found the right words.

Everyone in the class knew I'd been doing their work as well as mine, yet it took me a while to realise it: I felt as though I'd taken at least forty-five minutes of our time in a self-indulgent exercise. I couldn't have been more wrong. In our different ways we'd all experienced misdirected responsibility and each of us had been carrying it for a lifetime.

When we broke for lunch, Isabel took me

to one side and said, 'As soon as Mike said pick someone to play your mother, I was preparing myself. I was hoping you would choose me because I knew I could help you.' I asked her how she knew what to say. 'You told me when you said your parents had killed themselves. I understood why they'd done it.' Isabel had tapped into a mother's need to protect her child, but she didn't know that my mother had once said to a friend, 'I'm no good to Anna.' The words thank you didn't seem enough for everything Isabel had given me.

I felt as exhausted and elated as my father had when he made his descent from Mount Roraima, but without the torn and grimy khakis. He'd discovered prehistoric life 9,000 feet above sea level, while mine was confined well below ground. For both of us, it was a once-in-a-lifetime journey.

The next day, back in London, I noticed an immediate difference. I could breathe properly for the first time: deep, involuntary sighs of relief and release. I'd kept my emotions safely locked up in an oubliette of my own making, until Mike, Isabel, Ian and everyone on the course helped me find the key.

* * *

Even in absence, J. has been with me throughout this story. He knows my parents almost as well as I do, and more than once he's said, 'I could wring their bloody necks.' I used to feel the same way sometimes, but now that I understand why they had to leave me it's easier to bear. Having lived with a story that didn't sit right, both theirs and mine finally make sense.

I'd elevated J. to a level with my parents, and it took me four years, almost from the day I started writing this book to delivering the final draft, to finally allow him to take his rightful place. Despite his love and concern for my happiness, in the end he could only let me down. It was all so familiar, as if I had to come home in order to leave the past where it belongs. If I could find a way for us to be friends instead of lovers I would, but the risk is too great, inviting as it would all kinds of temptations and dangers. We last spoke about a month ago, and when I said goodbye I meant it.

★ ★ ★

Had my parents lived I'd be a very different person, and I'm not sure I would have liked her. When I said this out loud, all my friends understood. The one exception was an

314

acquaintance whose own relationship with his parents is fuelled by blame and resentment. 'What a dreadful thing to say,' he said. 'You can't possibly mean you're better off without your parents.' Yes, I do. I've had to rely on myself, and though the guidance might at times be impulsive or imprudent, the support is unwavering.

Alongside the disadvantages I've found more than a few benefits: I've never fallen out with my parents, or disappointed them and will never have to watch them deteriorate, helpless to prevent their slow decline. My father would be eighty-one now and my mother seventy-three, but they remain for ever young, their black and white photographs testament to unfinished lives.

When I wrote my first draft, I tried to present my parents in their best light because I wanted the reader to like them, but that's what Grandma and Gomez had done with my mother. Their tacit alliance produced a Disney adaptation so clean and shiny even she wouldn't have recognised it. As soon as I realised I was almost doing the same I changed tack and rewrote my parents as best I could in their true light. If I'm hard on them it's with reason and I'm harder on my mother because she had further to fall.

At the outset I thought this journey was

about love and forgiveness, but these are mere abstract nouns: I couldn't hold them in my hands, read them aloud or talk to them. In the end, I found there was nothing to forgive: my parents did the right thing when they left me. As for love, I have to admit there were times when I didn't even like them.

In conversation, aloud and to myself, I referred to my parents as my mother and father. Now, a sentence might flicker in my mind such as, 'My dad would have found that funny,' or 'I wish my mum could see this.' I'm aware of the possessive pronoun but in time I hope to think of them as plain old Mum and Dad.

Among my less pressing questions, I've always wanted to ask my parents why I was called Anna-Petra; it seemed like a mismatched pairing and I only use it in my signature. I'd solved one half of the riddle at sixteen when I read my father's novel, but Petra remained an enigma. Three days before I was due to deliver the manuscript to my editor, I received a call from a woman I'd been trying to locate for over a year. Rosamond Belfrage was my very last interview, she was also one of the people who looked after me when my mother was unable to cope towards the end of her marriage. Rosamond worked with my mother and Dot

Barclay at the Bureau of Hygiene and Tropical Medicine. Like Dot, she couldn't recall my mother ever mentioning her own writing. She did, however, remember a salient detail about my father's: 'Joan told me your father travelled to Petra a year or so before they met at Allington Castle. He was writing a book about it, but I'm not sure it was ever finished.'

Carved out of Jordan's pink sandstone and known as 'the rose-red city, half as old as time', Petra was the capital of the Nabataean Kingdom. During the second century AD, it disappeared from the map, lying dormant beneath the sand until it was rediscovered in 1812.

No one else has mentioned this book and it's not listed among my father's other titles in the British Library catalogue, nor at the Library of Congress. It would have been the last trip before his first suicide attempt, resulting in an unfinished manuscript no doubt thrown out when his bed-sit was cleared in 1968. Since Petra means rock, perhaps my father knew it would compensate for the fragility of *The Paradise Garden*'s Anna. Nice one Dad!

Aside from the fact my father left behind so much more than my mother, both in his writing and my own memories, his presence has always been easier to grasp. I had to dream the sound of her voice or try to replicate it with my own, but my father had two voices. As a child I had no trouble understanding 'Swanese'. Our vocabularies were on a par at some point, but I wonder when mine overtook his. I suspect at around the age of three. I'd never heard him speak in complete and eloquent sentences, though they may well have been perfectly formed in his brain. After his first suicide attempt, his synapses were misfiring and his speech a disjointed assemblage of vaguely related words. Not surprisingly, it was Henry James who brought my father into my living room.

Like a ghostly envoy, James crops up in my research as frequently as he did in my father's writing. In light of his regard for the Master, I've even given in to the italicised term, seeking precision in a desire to do justice to the meticulous in both of them.

I knew the chances of my father's radio broadcasts surviving the BBC's archival abolition of the 1970s were slim, wiped or binned to make space as so many tapes were. Of around forty programmes he made between 1946 and 1957, only one escaped the purge. Owing to BBC bureaucracy, it was nearly a year before I received a copy of 'Recollections of Henry James'. In 1956 my father recorded the memories of almost everyone alive who had known James. Interviewees included Max Beerbohm, Lady Violet Bonham-Carter, Sir Compton Mackenzie, Miss Bosanquet, the secretary, and Burgess Noakes, the valet, former bantam weight boxing champion of Sussex and, from the age of fourteen, devoted servant.

I'd waited so long to hear my father's true voice and when I did I burst out laughing — he sounded like Alistair Cooke impersonating Mr Cholmondley-Warner: it was 1950s BBC Received Pronunciation to a T. As I played the tape, I was aware of my father silently nodding as his interviewees related their first-hand stories of James. Needless to say, one of his first questions related to James's ponderous and measured speech, in which the pause was as resonant as the monologue he would eventually deliver to an audience patiently awaiting *les mots juste*.

As my father wrote in *Ilex and Olive*, he was unable to live completely in the world of his time. The eras and sensibilities he and James inhabited were two generations apart, yet I see a parallel in their last years, though James died at seventy-three and my father at forty-four. Towards the end of his life James suffered a series of strokes; he was partially paralysed and his speech more pause than words. Recalling how fastidious the Master was about his appearance, his valet said that even after his death he would have wanted to be presentable when the doctor arrived: 'There was one last service I was able to render Mr James — I shaved him just after he passed away.' My father died alone in the early hours of the morning in a squalid bed-sit. If I could, I would have straightened his collar and combed his hair.

He couldn't teach me much when he was alive, but I've learned at least one valuable lesson: the art of listening without interruption or impatience. His last surviving sibling, Pauline, is now ninety-three. Her memory remains sharp but certain stories recur like a tic. When she said for the third time: 'Did I tell you about Aunt Eva?' I didn't say, 'Yes, Pauline, twice already,' I let her talk. Eva was a funny one. Envious of her sister Gwendolyn's happy marriage to Topsy, she inherited what was left of the Hyde-Clarke fortune and was a spinster until her late forties.

Eventually, Pauline remembered why her name kept coming up: 'Aunt Eva . . . married her first cousin . . . two days after the wedding she jumped through a window.' Dotty Aunt Frances gassed herself eight years later. My father's intrigue for his eccentric maiden aunt may well have been more than casual curiosity.

It seems bad blood runs in both sides of my family. My mother's younger sister Susan overdosed on pills and alcohol in 1975, as did my cousin Amanda three years ago. All of them left young children. In therapeutic parlance, this psychogenic pattern is known as 'familial transmission', meaning the unconscious communication of a previous generation's trauma. Its signal, however, is picked up only by those with an inherent antenna. Thankfully, I'm tuned into a different station.

When my aunt, Marsli, recently told me Grandma wanted me to be a little version of my mother, I shuddered. I think Grandma always knew I could no more take on the role than I could pass another maths exam. Not long after I went to Christ's Hospital, I began my exit, stage left, from her psychodrama. By fourteen, after the first spinal surgery scare, I wanted no part in it. At eighteen, I joined a company of healthier and much happier families than ours.

My grandparents moved back to Merthyr in 1979. When Grandma died two years later, I felt guilty and thoroughly ungrateful. Now I know that my withdrawal from her over-protective arms was an act of self-preservation. Perhaps she was living up to the name of her home town, since Merthyr is Welsh for martyr, and too close a word to 'victim' for me.

Living on his own, with a diet of kippers, Madeira cake and ginger beer, Grandpa seemed to perk up. When I went to visit him in his flat on the outskirts of town, he was keeping company with an assembly of pastel-coloured miniature budgies. He told me the blue one was called Joey. And the pink, green and yellow ones? 'Joey,' he said with a rascally grin. He was a regular customer at the pet shop, but after a few months the manager became suspicious. Twenty or so birds later, Grandpa eventually admitted that a succession of Joeys had choked on his pipe smoke. Following his confession, he was banned from the pet shop.

When he moved into a nursing home at eighty-seven, many of the residents were his childhood friends from Toyn. The nurses said he was the life and soul, with an endless repertoire of naughty stories and saved up mischievous moments. During his last few years Grandpa was happily back in 'God's pocket'.

★ ★ ★

One of my last ports of call in my research was to send samples of my parents' handwriting and mine to a graphologist for analysis. Based only on our letters and dates of birth, Deborah Jaffe's report was chillingly accurate. It confirmed much of what I'd discovered but also revealed a few insights I'd missed.

If typography is the text's faithful servant, penmanship is the impostor's nemesis: 'No one can hide behind their handwriting,' Deborah said. 'Even if you try to disguise it you give yourself away.' As unique as a fingerprint, our handwriting is a calligraphic self-portrait. Both an art and a science, graphology's lexicon of terms, such as garlands and arcades, trails and vectors, gauge and currency, convey both mystery and method.

After studying Deborah's analysis I realised I might have saved myself about 70 per cent of my research, but as she said when we met, 'You prefer to do things the hard way.' Written in the present tense, her observations read as though my parents are still here, but it's my mother who is living in the moment as if there were no tomorrow.

Joan Swan: The swiftness in her soaring strokes indicates a quick thinker with a need to get her thoughts down fast, as if she has a lot to say in a short time. Her senses are highly developed. She finds great comfort in music, and has an eye for detail and colour and would take pleasure in embroidery. She is very creative but lacks confidence in her abilities, and doesn't feel the need to be acknowledged for herself. Her fantasies and desires are unfulfilled, and her sexual nature is either suppressed or not recognised. It's as if she's placed in the wrong time, a bloom growing in a cold climate. Had she been born thirty years later she would have blossomed. Her antenna is alert but she's unable to switch off from an over-fertile imagination.

She knows how to act in any given situation; you could take her anywhere in society and she'd blend in. She is congenial and not inclined to impose her views or opinions on others. Contemplative and a dreamer, her aspirations are often idealistic. She allows very few people to get close to her on an emotional level, yet protects her loved ones. She has a sympathetic nature and given far more of herself to others than she is prepared to take from them.

Michael Swan: This character speaks and writes with his mind not his heart, and internalises his feelings, an attitude he feels is a masculine approach. His capacity for memorising facts and information is formidable. He is prone to compulsive behaviour, yet discreet and respectful to those who confide in him. He is modest and self-effacing, almost to a fault, but suffers from shame, particularly related to certain events in his childhood which he understands but cannot easily accept.

Anna Swan: The pressure of her pen means she follows things through, sustains her ideas and goals and won't give up until she achieves them. Her inner critic is hard to please, like her father's, and she is susceptible to other people's opinions of her work or those who might want to stall her progress. She likes the risk of a stimulating challenge, whether it's a person or a task, but she needs to know when to walk away from it as it will affect her well-being and drain her of energy. She expects others to be reliable and dependable, and when they let her down the disappointment is hard to accept; she expects too much of them at times. A realist but no conformist, her actions sometimes get her into trouble. Unlike her parents', Anna's persona, or mask, shows very little discrepancy between her true self and the one she presents to the world. Direct in her communications, she has strong opinions and can be a little tactless.

When we met to go through her report, I found that Deborah is as much life coach as graphologist. She gave me a thorough talking to about the stimulating challenge; having spent four long years with my parents, and with J., I already knew it was time to walk away. As for my inner critic — made up of Gomez, Fatty M. and one or two others whose judgements no longer count — I've told it to bugger off.

Deborah's final observation related to the slant of my parents' script. 'Your father's leans to the right and indicates a paternal influence, your mother's to the left revealing an ingrained maternal dominance,' she said. 'Now look at yours.' I looked at the letter I'd written and smiled to myself. I'm happy to say that my handwriting is, and always will be, straight up and rock steady.

Postscript

I've spent my life measuring history by two dates — 1957 and 1962, the years of my father's first suicide attempt and my mother's death — and by two ages, thirty-one and forty-four. I'm now a month past my forty-fourth birthday. It's time I stopped measuring.

Early last summer, I planted two lavender bushes side by side for my parents. It's now mid January and I just went out to my garden to check on them. The jasmine and climbing clematis are resting until spring but the lavenders are flourishing — luscious green and wet with rain. I'm writing this with their scent on my fingertips.

We do hope that you have enjoyed reading this large print book.

Did you know that all of our titles are available for purchase?

We publish a wide range of high quality large print books including:
**Romances, Mysteries, Classics
General Fiction
Non Fiction and Westerns**

Special interest titles available in large print are:
**The Little Oxford Dictionary
Music Book
Song Book
Hymn Book
Service Book**

Also available from us courtesy of Oxford University Press:
**Young Readers' Dictionary
(large print edition)
Young Readers' Thesaurus
(large print edition)**

For further information or a free brochure, please contact us at:
**Ulverscroft Large Print Books Ltd.,
The Green, Bradgate Road, Anstey,
Leicester, LE7 7FU, England.
Tel:** (00 44) 0116 236 4325
Fax: (00 44) 0116 234 0205

JUST A BOY

Richard McCann

Richard McCann was just five when his mother became the first victim of Peter Sutcliffe, the man who came to be known as the 'Yorkshire Ripper'. He and his three sisters, forced to return to their estranged father, were never allowed to heal or forget, their grief caught up in the media circus of a serial killer. Yet Richard and his eldest sister Sonia were forced to endure violent abuse and keep the silence of forgotten children. This is the moving and inspirational story of how two small children stuck together through unimaginable pain and just when they hit rock-bottom, on the road to ruining their own lives forever, decided to make a change.

TWO STEPS BACKWARD

Susie Kelly

Susie Kelly and her husband Terry dreamed of a home in France. With their dogs, parrots and horses, they moved to a farmhouse in the Poitou-Charentes region. While Terry worked in England, Susie had to contend with a homicidal gas cooker, burst pipes and a biting guinea fowl. The enormity of what they had taken on seemed overwhelming, and when Terry came close to death, the dream threatened to turn into a nightmare. But the kindness of the local community inspired them to make a new life for themselves in the place they now call home.

THE TERMINAL MAN

Sir Alfred Mehran/Andre Donkin

Mehran Karimi Nasseri, better known as 'Sir Alfred', has been living in the departure lounge of Terminal 1 of Charles de Gaulle Airport, Paris, for sixteen years. He sleeps on a bench, dines at McDonalds, and is surrounded by piles of magazines and his extensive diary. He arrived at the airport on 8th August 1988, intending to take a plane to London. Without the proper documentation he quickly found himself trapped in a bureaucratic catch-22 nightmare. Fearing arrest as an illegal immigrant if he left the terminal building, he has been waiting while lawyers and government officials argued about his case. This is his incredible story in his own words.